Praise for
Mastering Partial Least Squares Structural
Equation Modeling (PLS-SEM)
with SmartPLS in 38 Hours

"PLS-SEM is a very robust and advanced technique that is well suited for prediction in multi-equation econometric models. This easy-to-read book helps researchers apply various statistical procedures in SmartPLS quickly in a step-by-step manner. I would highly recommend it to all PLS-SEM user."

— Prof. Dipak C. Jain
President (European) and Professor of Marketing
CEIBS, Shanghai

"Having supervised to completion twenty-seven doctoral candidates, of which 70% utilized quantitative methodology using PLS, I wish I had Dr. Wong's book earlier. *Mastering Partial Least Squares Structural Equation Modeling (PLS-SEM) with SmartPLS in 38 Hours* provides all the essentials in comprehending, assimilating, applying and explicitly presenting sophisticated structured models in the most simplistic manner for a plethora of Business and Non-Business disciplines. Since PLS-SEM quantitative analysis has gained prominence with most top tiered academic journals, this book is a necessity for aspiring academics who wish to have prolific publications in highly ranked publications."

— Prof. Siva Muthaly
Dean, Faculty of Business & Management
Asia Pacific University of Technology & Innovation, Malaysia

"In a world filled with fake-news, academic research results get ever more important. For that reason, key methodologies like PLS-SEM must become available and understood beyond an elite scholar group. Dr. Wong's book does just that and is therefore highly recommended."

— Prof. dr. Jack AA van der Veen
Professor of Supply Chain Management
Nyenrode Business Universiteit, The Netherlands

"We teach PLS-SEM as part of our Marketing Research course at Seneca and Ken was able to turn this difficult subject into an easy one for our students. Researchers at all levels would definitely benefit from this well-organized book to become competent in this multivariate data analysis method."

— **Chris McCracken**
Academic Chair, School of Marketing
Seneca College, Canada

"A must-have edition for academics and practitioners alike. Dr. Wong brings a refreshing approach to this important topic supporting a wider application across sectors. The clarity of the content will encourage those new to the field to enhance their skill set with step-by-step support. The comprehensiveness of the edition will allow it to also serve as a valuable reference for even the most advanced researchers."

— **Prof. Margaret D. Osborne**
Former Academic Chair, School of Marketing
Seneca College, Canada

"Ken Wong has created an easy-to-use, all-in-one blueprint for academics and practitioners on PLS-SEM."

— **Prof. Seung Hwan (Mark) Lee**
Interim Director
Ted Rogers School of Retail Management
Ryerson University, Canada

"Finally, a step-by-step guide to one of the most used methods in academia. Life would be much easier for many of us. A must for anyone wanting to know it — well."

— **Prof. Terence Tse**
Associate Professor of Finance
ESCP Europe Business School, UK

"The new book of Dr. Ken Wong on PLS-SEM is a good contribution to help researchers in the application of this important tool in marketing research. His lucid writing style and useful illustrations make life simple for students, researchers and practitioners alike. Strongly recommended!"

— **Prof. Kanishka Bedi**
Professor, School of Business and Quality Management
Hamdan Bin Mohammed Smart University, UAE

"In real world scenarios, researchers as well as practising managers have always struggled with actual data that does not mimic the properties of a statistically normal distribution. Ken's graphic attempt proposing PLS-SEM as a possible alternate solution to identify complex causal relationships is indeed noteworthy, more so due to the book's hands on approach in using software with enough downloadable data sets to aid the familiarisation process without overwhelming the reader."

— **Prof. Chinmoy Sahu**
Dean, Manipal GlobalNxt University, Malaysia

Mastering Partial Least Squares Structural Equation Modeling (PLS-SEM) with SmartPLS in 38 Hours

Mastering Partial Least Squares Structural Equation Modeling (PLS-SEM) with SmartPLS in 38 Hours

KEN KWONG-KAY WONG
Co-founder of Presentria

MASTERING PARTIAL LEAST SQUARES STRUCTURAL EQUATION MODELING (PLS-SEM) WITH SMARTPLS IN 38 HOURS

iUniverse books may be ordered through booksellers or by contacting:

iUniverse
1663 Liberty Drive
Bloomington, IN 47403
www.iuniverse.com
1-800-Authors (1-800-288-4677)

ISBN: 978-1-5320-6649-8 (sc)
ISBN: 978-1-5320-6648-1 (e)

Library of Congress Control Number: 2019900937

Print information available on the last page.

iUniverse rev. date: 02/21/2019

BRIEF CONTENTS

TABLE OF CONTENTS

ALSO BY KEN K. WONG

Approved Marketing Plans for New Products and Services

*Avoiding Plagiarism: Write Better Papers in APA,
Chicago, and Harvard Citation Styles*

*CRM in Action: Maximizing Value Through Market
Segmentation, Product Differentiation & Customer Retention*

*More Bucks Annually: Insider's Guide to Getting
Your MBA, DBA, and PhD Online*

*Putting a Stake in the Ground: Strategies for Getting Your
First Marketing Journal Article Published Successfully*

To my wife Winnie, my daughter Lydia, and my family members Hello Ma, Hello Dad, and Hello Chiu

Thank you for your love, understanding, patience, and confidence.

FOREWORD

This book clearly demonstrates Dr. Ken Wong's expertise in the field of PLS-SEM. His work broadens and strengthens the advanced statistical skills of researchers and practitioners. Readers who are eager to explore this subject would benefit from this refreshing step-by-step guide and be able to elevate their analytical skills. I have thoroughly reviewed this textbook and highly recommend it to the scholars.

Alireza Faed, Ph.D (Curtin)
Professor, School of Marketing
Seneca College of Applied Arts and Technology

PREFACE

Partial Least Squares Structural Equation Modeling (PLS-SEM)[1] is a second-generation multivariate statistical procedure that can be applied in marketing research (Biong & Ulvnes, 2011; Hair, Sarstedt, Ringle, & Mena, 2012; Wong, 2010, 2016). This variance-based SEM method is a great way to estimate complex interrelationships simultaneously and is well-known for its ability to make prediction in success factor studies (Albers, 2010; Rigdon, 2014). PLS-SEM can accommodate both formative[2] and reflective[3] measurement model types. Unlike Jöreskog's (1973) covariance-based SEM (CB-SEM) that is built upon a common factor model, PLS-SEM follows a composite model approach in construct measures estimation (Lohmöller, 1989). As such, it is great for measuring not only effect indicators[4] in reflective measuring model, but also composite indicators[5] in a formative measurement model. With correct specification, PLS-SEM can be used to approximate formative measurement model that consists of causal indicators as well (Sarstedt, Hair, Ringle, Thiele, & Gudergan, 2016).

---

[1] PLS-SEM is also known as PLS path modeling in some literature.
[2] In a Formative measurement model, the indicators are not closely correlated and not interchangeable. Two types of indicators exist in this formative model, namely causal indicators and composite indicators (Bollen, 2011; Bollen & Bauldry, 2011).
[3] In a Reflective measurement models, the indicators are highly correlated and interchangeable.
[4] Effect indicators are also known as Reflective indicators, they form a representative sample of all possible items available in the construct's conceptual domain (Nunnally & Bernstein, 1994).
[5] Indicators are also known as manifest variables or items.

Researchers have increasingly turned to PLS-SEM for business research (Hair, Sarstedt, Pieper, & Ringle, 2012; Carrion, Henseler, Ringle, & Roldan, 2016) and this statistical procedure has been adopted by science researchers as well (Hsu, Chang, & Lai, 2016; Jisha, & Thomas, 2016; Kansky, Kidds, & Knight, 2016). A wide range of software can be used to perform PLS path modeling (Wong, 2010) but one called SmartPLS (Ringle, Wende, & Becker, 2015) has gained popularity in recent years. Version 3 of this software has introduced new features that help researchers to automatic some statistical procedures that could only be performed manually in the previous versions.

Despite the hard work put forth by PLS-SEM researchers, the amount of literature on these emerging topics is still limited and they have not yet been fully covered by major research textbooks. Many of my Masters, PhD and DBA students still find the existing journal articles and books difficult to comprehend, especially when their dissertation-writing deadlines are fast approaching. To make it worse, some of their supervisors have never dealt with PLS-SEM before, making it even more difficult for these poor students to learn this wonderful data analysis methodology.

This book fills the gap by demonstrating through marketing-related examples how SmartPLS can be used practically in both version 2 and 3 of the software. Advanced techniques such as Confirmatory Tetrad Analysis (CTA-PLS), Quadratic Effect Modeling (QEM), Heterogeneity Modeling, Higher Order Construct Modeling (HCM), Mediation Analysis, and Categorical Moderation Analysis (PLS-MGA) are explained in a step-by-step manner to help researchers master these techniques confidently.

The PLS-SEM field has progressed significantly in the past few years with substantial development of new techniques. For example, we can now obtain better results for reflective models using Consistent PLS (PLSc), assess discriminant validity using Heterotrait-Monotrait Ratio of Correlations (HTMT), contrast total effects using Importance-Performance Matrix Analysis (IPMA), test goodness of model fit using Standardized Root Mean Squared Residual (SRMR), Unweighted Least Squares Discrepancy (d_{ULS}) and Geodesic Discrepancy (d_G). All of these latest developments have taken PLS-SEM to the next level and are discussed in Chapter 12.

You can download the dataset free of charge from www.presentria.ca to work along the examples. Regarding the book title, I have chosen to mention "38 hours" because that is the duration of my popular PLS-SEM research module. If my students can master this subject well in 38 hours, so can you! I hope you would find my work interesting and beneficial to your research project. Finally, to those soon-to-be Masters/PhDs/DBAs, "Good luck with your dissertation!"

Dr. Ken Kwong-Kay Wong

Toronto, Ontario, Canada
February 12, 2019

E-mail: ken.wong@utoronto.ca

Web: www.presentria.ca
Research Gate: http://www.researchgate.net/profile/Ken_Wong10
Google Scholar: http://scholar.google.ca/
    citations?user=zaEmJgUAAAAJ&hl=en
LinkedIn: https://ca.linkedin.com/in/ken-kwong-kay-wong-893490
RateMyProfessor (Ryerson): http://www.ratemyprofessors.com/
    ShowRatings.jsp?tid=1751501
RateMyProfessor (Seneca): http://www.ratemyprofessors.com/
    ShowRatings.jsp?tid=2056117

ABOUT THE AUTHOR

Dr. Ken Kwong-Kay Wong is a full-time, tenured marketing professor at Seneca College in Toronto. Since 2003, he has taught marketing to over 6,000 working professionals at the University of Toronto's School of Continuing Studies. Ken has taught marketing research for 16 years, including the RMG700 Applied Retail Research course at Ryerson University and the MRK455 Applied Marketing Research course at Seneca Business. He also co-founded Presentria to make inclusive teaching and learning a reality through the use of Artificial Intelligence (AI), Internet of Things (IoT), Location-based Services (LBS), and other advanced computing technologies.

Ken enjoys inspiring MBAs and senior executives around the world. He was a visiting professor at the "Triple Crown" accredited Aalto University (Finland, South Korea, and Taiwan) and Hult International Business School (USA, UAE and China), the AMBA and EQUIS-accredited

Nyenrode Business Universiteit (The Netherlands), the ACBSP-accredited International School of Management (France), and the AMBA-accredited COTRUGLI Business School (Bulgaria, Croatia, and Romania). He has trained Deutsche Telekom managers on social media and LG Electronics engineers and managing directors on customer experience management.

A retail expert known to the business community, Ken previously served as an Assistant Professor in Retail Management at the AACSB-accredited Ryerson University, where he received the 2014 and 2015 "A Prof Who Made a Mark" award. He also worked as a Marketing Professor and Subject Area Coordinator at the EFMD-accredited U21Global from 2006 to 2012, where he received the Outstanding Professor, Most Innovative Professor, and Excellence in Online Education awards. His research interests include luxury marketing, customer experience management, and emerging research methods such as PLS-SEM. He has published 18 peer-reviewed publications and 7 trade books.

Prior to entering the academic field, Ken was the Vice President of Marketing at TeraGo Networks (TSX: TGO) and had previously served as the Director of Product Marketing at PSINet (NASDAQ: PSIX). He had also held progressive product marketing roles at Sprint Canada (TSX: FON) and TELUS Mobility (TSX: T).

Ken received a DBA from the University of Newcastle, Australia in 2006, an MBA from Nyenrode Business Universiteit in the Netherlands in 1998, and a BSc from the University of Toronto in 1997. He was certified by the American Marketing Association in 2002 as a Professional Certified Marketer (PCM).

ACKNOWLEDGEMENTS

I would like to acknowledge my gratitude to Prof. dr. ir. Jörg Henseler (University of Twente, Enschede), whose comments resulted in a notable improvement of this book. I also want to thank my colleagues and friends who reviewed my work during their busy schedule.

Reviewers for this Edition:

Prof. Dipak C. Jain, CEIBS, China
Prof. Paul Lam, The Chinese University of Hong Kong, China
Prof. Mark Esposito, Harvard University, USA
Prof. Terence Tse, ESCP Europe Business School, UK
Prof. dr. Jack AA van der Veen, Nyenrode Business Universiteit, The Netherlands
Dean Jan Goedvolk, Hult International Business School, UAE/China
Dean Luis Escamilla, Hult International Business School, UAE/USA
Dean Siva Muthaly, Asia Pacific University of Technology & Innovation, Malaysia
Dean Chinmoy Sahu, Manipal GlobalNxt University, Malaysia
Dean Mary Vaughan, Seneca College, Canada
Chris McCracken, BAA, Seneca College, Canada
Sarah Arliss, MA, Seneca College, Canada
Margaret Osborne, MBA, Seneca College, Canada
Dr. Alireza Faed, Seneca College, Canada
Dr. Reid Kerr, Seneca College, Canada
Dr. Rita Obaji, Seneca College, Canada
Dr. Maksim Sokolov, Seneca College, Canada
Prof. Murtaza Haider, Ryerson University, Canada

Prof. Seung Hwan (Mark) Lee, Ryerson University, Canada
Prof. Hong Yu, Ryerson University, Canada
Prof. Osmud Rahman, Ryerson University, Canada
Prof. Norman Shaw, Ryerson University, Canada
Dr. Janice Rudkowski, Ryerson University, Canada
Sean Sedlezky, MScM, Ryerson University, Canada
Prof. Mamata Bhandar, Manipal GlobalNxt University, Malaysia
Prof. Amy Wong, Singapore University of Social Sciences, Singapore
Prof. Kanishka Bedi, Hamdan Bin Mohammed Smart University, UAE

CHAPTER 1

Introduction

The Research Dilemma

In any marketing research project, an ideal data set should have a large sample size and be normally distributed. Unfortunately, the reality is that many applied research projects have limited participants because of the nature of the project. Insufficient resources and tight project timelines further prevent researchers from obtaining a decent data set for proper statistical analysis, particularly in the structural equation modeling (SEM) of latent variables where LISREL (linear structural relations) and AMOS (analysis of moment structures) have strict data assumptions. Some researchers have taken the risk of drawing incorrect or limited inferences by ignoring the data set requirements, while others have resorted to testing simplified versions of complex hypotheses. This book introduces an emerging multivariate analysis approach called "partial least squares structural equation modeling" (PLS-SEM), which is a good solution to these problems, if it is used properly.

A Better Way to Measure Customer Satisfaction

Companies strive to increase their bottom-line performance through increasing customer satisfaction levels. However, a single question (e.g., Are you satisfied with our product?) may provide marketers with little value, because customer satisfaction is multi-dimensional, and this latent variable is not directly observable. A better way to measure satisfaction is to consider survey responses to several manifest variables on a continuous

1

(multi-point) scale. Marketers are often interested in identifying the key operational processes and product attributes that drive customer satisfaction so that they can prioritize resources to improve these areas. SEM is designed for testing theoretically supported linear and additive causal models. It is ideal for examining the relationship between customer satisfaction and other variables.

Different Approaches to SEM

There are several distinct approaches to SEM: The first approach is the widely applied Covariance-based SEM (CB-SEM)[6], using software packages such as AMOS, EQS, LISREL and MPlus. The second approach is Partial Least Squares (PLS), which focuses on the analysis of variance and can be carried out using ADANCO, PLS-Graph, VisualPLS, SmartPLS, and WarpPLS. It can also be employed using the PLS module in the "r" statistical software package. The third approach is a component-based SEM known as Generalized Structured Component Analysis (GSCA); it is implemented through VisualGSCA or a web-based application called GeSCA. Another way to perform SEM is called Nonlinear Universal Structural Relational Modeling (NEUSREL), using NEUSREL's Causal Analytics software.

Faced with various approaches to path modeling, one has to consider their advantages and disadvantages to choose an approach to suit.

CB-SEM

CB-SEM has been widely applied in the field of social science during the past several decades, and is still the preferred data analysis method today for confirming or rejecting theories through testing of hypothesis, particularly when the sample size is large, the data is normally distributed, and most importantly, the model is correctly specified. That is, the appropriate variables are chosen and linked together in the process of converting a theory into a structural equation model (Hair, Ringle, & Smarted, 2011; Hwang et al., 2010; Reinartz, Haenlein, & Henseler,

---

[6] Covariance-based SEM (CB-SEM) is also known as Covariance Structure Analysis (CSA)

2009). However, many industry practitioners and researchers note that, in reality, it is often difficult to find a data set that meets these requirements. Furthermore, the research objective may be exploratory, in which we know little about the relationships that exist among the variables. In this case, marketers can consider PLS.

PLS-SEM

PLS is a soft modeling approach to SEM with no assumptions about data distribution[7] (Vinzi et al., 2010). Thus, PLS-SEM becomes a good alternative to CB-SEM for many researchers. In reality, PLS is found to be useful for structural equation modeling in applied research projects, especially when there are limited participants and that the data distribution is skewed, e.g., surveying female senior executive or multinational CEOs (Wong, 2011). PLS-SEM has been deployed in many fields, such as behavioral sciences (e.g., Bass et al, 2003), marketing (e.g., Henseler et al., 2009), organization (e.g., Sosik et al., 2009), management information system (e.g., Chin et al., 2003), and business strategy (e.g., Hulland, 1999).

GSCA & Other Approaches

If overall measures of model fit are really important to the researcher, or in projects where many non-linear latent variables exist and have to be accommodated, GSCA may be a better choice than PLS for running structural equation modeling (Hwang et al., 2010). And for data sets that demonstrate significant nonlinearities and moderation effects among variables, the NEUSREL approach may be considered (Frank and Hennig-Thurau, 2008).

However, since GSCA and NEUSREL are relatively new approaches in SEM, the amount of literature for review is relatively limited. Marketers may find it difficult to locate sufficient examples to understand how these emerging SEM approaches can be used in different business research scenarios.

---

[7] However, with regard to assumptions made for the estimation of parameters, PLS-SEM is the same as other SEM techniques.

Why not LISREL or Amos?

Since the 1970s, marketers have used Scientific Software International's LISREL and SmallWaters/SPSS's Amos statistical software packages to build causal models. Although these covariance-based SEM software packages are great for estimating and testing model parameters using maximum likelihood, they have some disadvantages from a user's perspective. For example, a large sample size of 500 or more participants is usually required to generate stable estimation of the parameters. The dataset has to be normally distributed, or else standard errors must be used with care when the assumptions of multivariate normality are not met. The researcher also needs at least three manifest variables per latent variable to avoid identification problems.

The Birth of PLS-SEM

In the mid-1960s, the renowned econometrician and statistician Herman Wold developed the concept of a predictive causal system called "partial least squares." This new variance-based SEM approach extended the principal component and canonical correlation analysis to the next level. Unlike LISREL or AMOS, it is designed to provide flexibility for exploratory modeling. PLS is well known for its soft modeling approach, using ordinary least squares (OLS) multiple regression, which makes no distributional assumptions in computation of the model parameters. Because PLS fits each part of the model separately, it reduces the number of cases required. However, please note that a larger sample size always helps to improve parameter estimation and reduce average absolute error rates. PLS favours the outer measurement model that deals with the relations between latent variables and their manifest variables. Statistically speaking, the objective of PLS is to get score values of latent variables for prediction purposes. It is a component-based technique in which latent variables are calculated as exact weighted linear combinations of the manifest variables. This methodology is called "partial" least squares because its iterative procedure involves separating the parameters instead of estimating them simultaneously. Key resampling procedures include bootstrapping, jackknifing and blindfolding.

Growing Acceptance of PLS-SEM

Although PLS was developed more than five decades ago, it did not gain the attention of the academic community until the late 1990s, because of a lack of PLS software and documentation. In the last two decades, the situation has improved significantly with the launch of graphical PLS software such as PLS-Graph, VisualPLS, SmartPLS, WarpPLS, and ADANCO. The first international PLS conference was conducted in 1999, and the first PLS handbook was published by Springer in 2010. With increased use of the PLS method in top-tier, peer-reviewed journal papers (particularly in the Journal of Management Information Systems) and in the marketing and behavioural science fields, it is a good time to give this innovative approach serious consideration. As PLS has been utilized by researchers in many studies based on the American Customer Satisfaction Index (ACSI), having a good understanding of PLS methodology helps researchers to compare their research results with those of prior studies.

Strengths of PLS-SEM

A substantial amount of research on the benefits of the PLS path modelling approach has been published (Bacon, 1999; Hwang et al., 2010; Wong, 2010). Among these benefits are the following:

- Small sample size requirement[8]
- Hypotheses that are less probabilistic
- No assumptions about the distribution of the variables
- Insensitivity to non-normality, heteroscedasticity, and autocorrelation of the error terms
- No parameter identification problem
- No need for observations to be independent
- Ability to explore the relationship between a latent variable and its manifest variables in both formative and reflective ways
- Effectiveness in analysing moderation effects and identification of potential moderators

---

[8] PSL-SEM can handle large sample size as well. For inference statistics, researchers should make sure sufficient statistical power and representativeness of data.

- Production of scores both for overall and for individual cases
- Ability to handle large model complexity (up to 100 latent and 1,000 manifest variables)
- Suitability for research when improper or non-convergent results are likely.

Weaknesses of PLS-SEM

Marketing researchers are urged to evaluate PLS's strengths and weaknesses carefully before adopting the approach. As experts would agree, there is no magic bullet in any particular statistical procedure. Among the weaknesses of PLS are the following:

- Requirement for high-valued structural path coefficients when using small sample sizes
- Inability to handle the multicollinearity problem well
- Inability to provide ways of modelling undirected correlation
- Possibility of resulting in biased estimates of component loadings and path coefficients, due to a lack of complete consistency in scores on latent variables
- Possible generation of large mean square errors of loading estimates and large mean square errors of path coefficient estimates.

Evolution of PLS-SEM Software

Although developed in the mid-1960s (Wold, 1973, 1985), there has been a lack of advanced yet easy-to-use PLS path modeling software (not to be confused with PLS regression as it is different from PLS-SEM) until mid 2000s. The first generation of PLS-SEM software that was commonly used in the 1980s included LVPLS 1.8, but it was a DOS-based program. The subsequent arrival of PLS-Graph and VisualPLS added a graphical interface but they have received no significant updates since their initial releases. PLS-SEM can be performed in "r" but it requires certain level of programming knowledge. Therefore, it may not be suitable for those marketers who do not have strong computer science background. The remaining standalone PLS-SEM software packages, still in active development, include ADANCO, SmartPLS, and WarpPLS. Please refer to Chapter 13 for a full list of available PLS-related software packages.

This book focuses on SmartPLS because it is widely used in the academic community. This software not only releases updates regularly, but also maintains an active online discussion forum[9], providing a good platform for knowledge exchange among its users.

---

[9] Online forum is located at the developer's web site (http://forum.smartpls.com).

CHAPTER 2

Understanding the PLS-SEM Components

Inner (Structural) and Outer (Measurement) Models

Partial Least Squares Structural Equation Modeling (PLS-SEM) is a second-generation multivariate data analysis method that is often used in marketing research because it can test theoretically supported linear and additive causal models (Chin, 1996; Haenlein & Kaplan, 2004; Statsoft, 2013). With PLS-SEM, marketers can visually examine the relationships that exist among variables of interest in order to prioritize resources to better serve their customers. The fact that unobservable, hard-to-measure latent variables[10] can be used in SEM makes it ideal for tackling business research problems.

There are two sub-models in a structural equation model; the inner model[11] specifies the relationships between the independent and dependent latent variables, whereas the outer model[12] specifies the relationships between the latent variables and their observed indicators[13] (see Figure 1). In SEM, a variable is either exogenous or endogenous. An exogenous variable has path arrows pointing outwards and none leading to it. Meanwhile, an

---

[10] Latent variables are underlying variables that cannot be observed directly, they are also known as constructs or factors.

[11] The inner model is also known as a structural model.

[12] The outer model is also known as a measurement model.

[13] Observed indicators can be measured directly, they act as indicators for an underlying latent variable.

endogenous variable[14] has at least one path leading to it and represents the effects of other variable(s).

Figure 1: Inner vs. Outer Model in a PLS-SEM Diagram

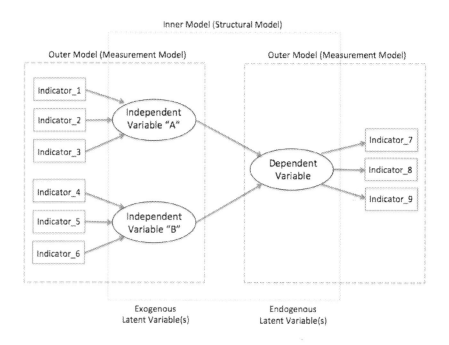

Determination of Sample Size in PLS-SEM

No matter which PLS-SEM software is being used, some general guidelines should be followed when performing PLS path modeling. This is particularly important, as PLS is still an emerging multivariate data analysis method, making it easy for researchers, academics, or even journal editors to let inaccurate applications of PLS-SEM go unnoticed. Determining the appropriate sample size is often the first headache faced by researchers.

---

[14] Depending on the SEM design, a variable can technically act as an independent variable or a dependent variable for different parts of the model; as long as a variable has path leading to it (i.e., arrows pointing to it from another variable), it is categorized as endogenous.

In general, one has to consider the background of the model, the distributional characteristics of the data, the psychometric properties of variables, and the magnitude of their relationships when determining sample size. Hair et al. (2013) suggest that sample size can be driven by the following factors in a structural equation model design:

1. The significance level
2. The statistical power
3. The minimum coefficient of determination (R^2 values) used in the model
4. The maximum number of arrows pointing at a latent variable

In practice, a typical marketing research study would have a significance level of 5%, a statistical power of 80%, and R^2 values of at least 0.25. Using such parameters, the minimum sample size required can be looked up from the guidelines suggested by Marcoulides & Saunders (2006), depending on the maximum number of arrows pointing at a latent variable as specified in the structural equation model (see Figure 2):

Figure 2: Suggested Sample Size in a Typical Marketing Research

Minimum sample size required	Maximum # of arrows pointing at a latent variable in the model
52	2
59	3
65	4
70	5
75	6
80	7
84	8
88	9
91	10

Although PLS is well known for its capability of handling small sample sizes, it does not mean that your goal should be to merely fulfill the minimum sample size requirement. Prior research suggests that a sample size of 100 to 200 is usually a good starting point in carrying out path modeling (Hoyle, 1995). Please note that the required sample size will need to be increased if the research objective is to explore low-value factor intercorrelations with indicators that have poor quality.

Formative vs. Reflective Measurement Scale

There are two types of measurement scale in structural equation modeling; it can be formative or reflective.[15]

Formative Measurement Scale

If the indicators cause the latent variable and are not interchangeable among themselves, they are formative. In general, these formative indicators can have positive, negative, or even no correlations among each other (Haenlein & Kaplan, 2004; Petter et al., 2007). As such, there is no need to report indicator reliability, internal consistency reliability, and discriminant validity if a formative measurement scale is used. This is because outer loadings, composite reliability, and square root of average variance extracted (AVE) are meaningless for a latent variable made up of uncorrelated measures.

A good example of formative measurement scale is the measurement of employee's stress level. Since it is a latent variable that is often difficult to measure directly, researchers have to look at indicators that can be measured, such as divorce, job loss, and car accidents. Here, it is obvious that a car accident does not necessarily have anything to do with divorce or job loss, and these indicators are not interchangeable.

When formative indicators exist in the model, the direction of the arrows has to be reversed. That is, the arrow should be pointing from the yellow-color formative indicators to the blue-color latent variable in SmartPLS. This can be done easily by right clicking on the latent variable and selecting "Invert measurement model" to change the arrow direction.[16]

---

[15] Traditionally, we focus on deciding whether a model has "formative" or "reflective" measurement scale. However, the modern view of PLS-SEM looks at the model from the perspective of whether it is a "factor" or "composite" one. See Henseler, Hubona, and Ray (2016). In this book, we will follow the traditional view on this matter.

[16] This way of building a formative model is called "Mode B" in which regression weights are used to create the proxy.

Reflective Measurement Scale

If the indicators are highly correlated and interchangeable, they are reflective and their reliability and validity should be thoroughly examined (Haenlein & Kaplan, 2004; Hair et al., 2013; Petter et al., 2007). For example, in the next chapter, we will introduce you to a case study that is related to conducting survey in a restaurant. The latent variable Perceived Quality (QUAL) in our restaurant dataset is made up of three observed indicators[17]: food taste, server professionalism, and bill accuracy. Their outer loadings, composite reliability, AVE and its square root should be examined and reported.

In a reflective measurement scale, the causality direction is going from the blue-color latent variable to the yellow-color indicators. It is important to note that by default, SmartPLS assumes the indicators are reflective when the model is built, with arrows pointing away from the blue-color latent variable.[18] One of the common mistakes that researchers make when using SmartPLS is forgetting to change the direction of the arrows when the indicators are formative instead of reflective. Since all of the indicators in this restaurant example are reflective, there is no need to change the arrow direction.

Should it be Formative or Reflective?

In case you are not 100% sure if a measurement model should be reflective or formative, the Confirmatory Tetrad Analysis (CTA-PLS) can be performed to find it out quantitatively. A step-by-step guide for using this technique is presented in the Chapter 6 of this book.

Guidelines for Correct PLS-SEM Application

In relation to other path modeling approaches, PLS-SEM is still relatively new to many researchers. Through extensive critical reviews of

---

[17] As a best practice, researcher should aim to get at least 4 indicators for each latent variable. In this book, we only use 2 or 3 indicators for each latent variable in our examples for a simplified demonstration purpose.

[18] This way of building a reflective model is called "Mode A" in which correlation weights are used to create the proxy.

this methodology in the last several years, the academic community has developed some guidelines for correct PLS-SEM application. First of all, research should develop a model that is consistent with the theoretical knowledge currently available. As in other research projects, proper data screening should be performed to ensure accuracy of input. In order to determine the sample size necessary for adequate power (e.g., 0.8), the distributional characteristics of the data, the psychometric properties of variables, and the magnitude of the relationships between the variables have to be examined carefully.

Although PLS-SEM is well known for its ability to handle small sample sizes, that is not the case when moderately non-normal data are used, even if the model includes highly reliable indicators. As a result, researchers are strongly advised to check the magnitude of the standard errors of the estimates and calculate the confidence intervals for the population parameters of interest. If large standard errors and wide confidence intervals are observed, they are good indications that the sample size is not large enough for proper analysis. Prior research has indicated that a sample size of 100 to 200 is a good start in carrying out PLS procedures. The required sample size will further increase if you are examining low-value-factor intercorrelations with poor quality indicators.

PLS is still considered by many as an emerging multivariate data analysis method, and researchers are still exploring the best practices of PLS-SEM. Even so, some general guidelines have been suggested in the literature. Figure 3 displays some of guidelines that should be considered.

Figure 3: Some Guidelines on PLS Applications

Topics:	Suggestions:	References:
1. Overall model assessment	Test of model fit (estimated model): • SRMR < 95% bootstrap quantile • d_{ULS} < 95% bootstrap quantile • d_G < 95% bootstrap quantile Approximate model fit (estimated model): • SRMR < 0.08	Henseler, Hubona, Ray (2016)
2. Outer (Measurement) model assessment	Confirmatory composite and/or Factor analysis (saturated model): • SRMR < 95% bootstrap quantile • d_{ULS} < 95% bootstrap quantile • d_G < 95% bootstrap quantile Approximate model fit (saturated model): • SRMR < 0.08 Internal consistency reliability: • rho_A >0.7 • Cronbach's alpha > 0.7 Convergent validity: • AVE > 0.5 Discriminant validity: • HTMT significantly less than 1 • Fornell-Larcker criterion • Loadings exceed cross-loadings	Henseler, Hubona, Ray (2016)
	Outer model evaluation (reflective): • Report indicator loadings. Do not use Cronbach's alpha for internal consistency reliability. Outer model evaluation (formative): • Report indicator weights. To test the outer model's significance, report t-values, p-values and standard errors	Bagozzi and Yi (1988)
3. Inner (Structural) model assessment	Endogenous variables: • R^2 and adjusted R^2 Direct effects: • Path coefficient (absolute size and sign) • Significance (p-value and CI) • Effect size Indirect effects: • Coefficient (absolute size, sign) • Significance (p-value and CI) Total effects: • Coefficient (absolute size, sign) • Significance (p-value and CI)	Henseler, Hubona, Ray (2016)
4. Measurement scale	Avoid using a categorical scale in endogenous constructs	Hair et al. (2010)
5. Bootstrapping	Number of bootstrap "samples" should be 5000 and number of bootstrap "cases" should be the same as the number of valid observations	Hair et al. (2011)

CHAPTER 3

Using SmartPLS Software for Path Model Estimation

Introduction to the SmartPLS Software Application

There are currently different versions of SmartPLS in circulation. The previous version, 2.0M3, is a freeware that has all of the core functionalities for PLS-SEM. Although it is only available on the Windows platform, this freely available version 2 is still used by thousands of researchers around the world because it does not have any limitation on the dataset. Once activated, this software has to be renewed online every three months with a free software license key that is e-mailed by the SmartPLS team to the registered user.

The current release of SmartPLS is 3.2.8 (as of February 2019), it is compatible with both Windows and macOS platforms. As compared to version 2, it adds many new and exciting functionalities such as Confirmatory Tetrad Analysis (CTA-PLS), Quadratic Effect Modeling (QEM), Measurement Invariance of the Composite Models (MICOM), Permutation Test, Finite Mixture Partial Least Squares (FIMIX-PLS), PLS Prediction-oriented Segmentation (PLS-POS), Consistent PLS (PLSc), Heterotrait-Monotrait Ratio of Correlations (HTMT), Importance-Performance Matrix Analysis (IPMA), and Goodness of Model Fit (GoF): SRMR, d_{ULS}, and d_G testing procedures.

Version 3 has a free "Student" version and also a paid "Professional/ Enterprise" version. The student edition allows a maximum of 100 observations (rows) in the dataset and has limited algorithms and data export options as compared to the paid version.

Downloading and Installing the Software

To download SmartPLS version 2, please first go to https:// www.smartpls.com/smartpls2 to fill out a product registration form. An e-mail from the SmartPLS team will then be sent to the user with the download link together with a software license key. Again, this release only supports the Windows platform. Intel-based Apple Mac users who want to use version 2 should utilize visualization software[19] or Apple's own Bootcamp function to run SmartPLS under the Windows OS environment[20].

To download SmartPLS version 3, please go to https://www.smartpls. com/downloads. Microsoft Windows user should can choose to download either the "32-bit Installer" or the "64-bit Installer", depending on the user's computer system configuration. For Mac users, there are two pieces of software to download: (i) DMG Installer for SmartPLS and (ii) Java Runtime.

If you are an instructor trying to teach PLS-SEM using SmartPLS 3, please ask students to download the software at home or campus prior to attending your lecture. This software is over 60MB in file size and it can be slow to download if all students are trying to access the server at the same time.

Solving Software Installation Problem on Recent Macs

Most of my students who used the latest Macs (with macOS El Capitan 10.11, Sierra 10.12, High Sierra 10.13, or Mojave 10.14) have reported problems installing the SmartPLS software. After some investigations, it turned out that they either forgot to install the Java Runtime software as mentioned before or did not grant security permission for such software installation (see Figure 4).

---

[19] Examples include VMware Fusion, Parallels Desktop, and Oracle's VirtualBox.
[20] Examples include Windows XP, VISTA, 7, 8 and 10.

Figure 4: Security Permission Problem in macOS

To solve the permission problem, first go to the Apple menu and select "System Preferences…" Then, click the "Security & Privacy" icon and go to the "General" tab. Press the "Open Anyway" button where it says "SmartPLS" was blocked from opening because it is not from an identified developer (see Figure 5).

Figure 5: Security & Privacy Settings

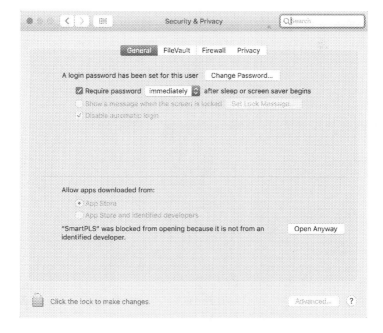

A pop-up window will appear to ask if you are sure that you want to open this SmartPLS software. Click the "Open" button to complete the installation process.

Case Study: Customer Survey in a Restaurant (B2C)

The following customer satisfaction example will be used to demonstrate how to use the SmartPLS software application.

Customer satisfaction is an example of a latent variable that is multidimensional and difficult to observe directly. However, one can measure it indirectly with a set of measurable indicators[21] that serve as proxy[22]. To understand customer satisfaction, a survey can be conducted to ask restaurant patrons about their dining experience. In this fictitious survey example, restaurant patrons are asked to rate their experience on a scale representing four latent variables, namely Customer Expectation (EXPECT), Perceived Quality (QUAL), Customer Satisfaction (SAT), and Customer Loyalty (LOYAL), using a 7-point Likert scales[23] [(1) *strongly disagree*, (2) *disagree*, (3) *somewhat disagree*, (4) *neither agree nor disagree*, (5) *somewhat agree*, (6) *agree*, and (7) *strongly agree*]. The conceptual framework is visually shown in Figure 6, and the survey questions asked are presented in Figure 7. Other than Customer Satisfaction (SAT) that is measured by one question, all other variables (QUAL, EXPECT, & LOYAL) are each measured by three questions. This design is in line with similar researches conducted for the retail industry (Hair et al., 2013).

[21] Indicators are also known as items or manifest variables.
[22] Categorical variables, including those "Yes/No" dichotomous ones, can be used in the model in theory, but researcher has to be careful when setting up such scale.
[23] An alternative approach is to use a 10-point Likert scale.

18

Figure 6: Conceptual Framework – Restaurant Example

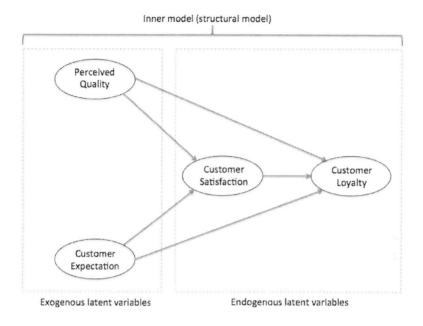

Figure 7: Questions for Indicator Variables

Customer Expectation (EXPECT)	
expect_1	[this restaurant] has the best menu selection.
expect_2	[this restaurant] has the great atmospheric elements.
expect_3	[this restaurant] has good looking servers.
Perceived Quality (QUAL)	
qual_1	The food in [this restaurant] is amazing with great taste.
qual_2	Servers in [this restaurant] are professional, responsive, and friendly.
qual_3	[this restaurant] provides accurate bills to customers.
Customer Satisfaction (SAT)	
cxsat	If you consider your overall experiences with [this restaurant], how satisfied are you with [this restaurant]?
Customer Loyalty (LOYAL)	
loyal_1	I would recommend [this restaurant] to my friends and relatives.
loyal_2	I would definitely dine at [this restaurant] again in the near future.
loyal_3	If I had to choose again, I would choose [this restaurant] as the venue for this dining experience.

Data Preparation for SmartPLS

In this restaurant example, the survey data were manually typed into Microsoft Excel and saved as *.xlsx* format (see Figure 8). This dataset has a sample size of 400 without any missing values, invalid observations or outliers. To ensure SmartPLS can import the Excel data properly, the names of those indicators (e.g., expect_1, expect 2, expect_3) should be placed in the first row of an Excel spreadsheet, and no "string" value (e.g., words or single dot[24]) should be used in other cells.

Figure 8 – Dataset from the Restaurant Example

	A	B	C	D	E	F	G	H	I	J
1	expect_1	expect_2	expect_3	cxsat	loyal_1	loyal_2	loyal_3	qual_1	qual_2	qual_3
2	2	6	5	6	2	6	7	5	4	2
3	3	5	4	5	3	5	5	2	1	2
4	7	7	7	7	7	7	7	7	7	7
5	4	4	5	6	5	6	6	5	2	3
6	5	7	6	7	7	7	7	6	6	3
7	7	7	7	7	7	7	7	7	7	7
8	7	5	7	7	7	7	7	4	1	7
9	6	6	6	4	5	4	6	4	3	4
10	5	7	6	6	5	7	7	7	5	7

Since SmartPLS cannot take native Excel file format directly, the dataset has to be converted into *.csv* file format[25]. To do this, go to the "File" menu in Excel, and choose "CSV (Comma Delimited)" as the file format type to save it onto your computer (see Figure 9).

---

[24] A single dot "." is usually generated by IBM SPSS Statistics to represent a missing value.

[25] SmartPLS can only open .csv or .txt file formats

Figure 9: Saving Data File in "CSV (Comma delimited)" Format

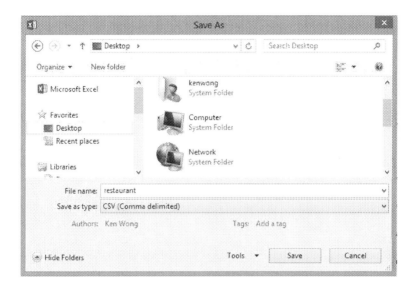

Project Creation in SmartPLS

Now, launch the SmartPLS program and go to the "File" menu to create a new project. We will name this project as "restaurant" and then import the indicator data. Since there is no missing value[26] in this restaurant data set, we can press the "Finish" button to create the PLS file. Once the data set is loaded properly into SmartPLS, click the little "+" sign next to restaurant to open up the data in the "Projects" tab (see Figure 10).

---

[26] For other data sets that include missing values, a replacement value of "-9999" is suggested. However, please note that you can only specify a single value for all missing data in SmartPLS.

Figure 10: Project Selection

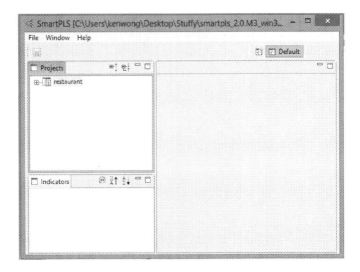

Under the "restaurant" project directory, a "restaurant.splsm" PLS file and a corresponding "restaurant.csv" data file are displayed[27]. Click on the first one to view the manifest variables under the "Indicators" tab (see Figure 11).

Figure 11: List of Indicators

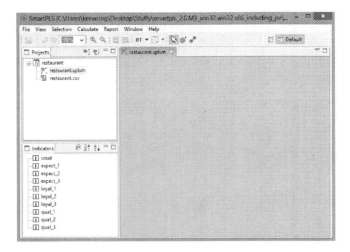

---

[27] For each project, you can have more than one path model (i.e., the .splsm file) and dataset (i.e., .csv file).

Building the Inner Models

Based on the conceptual framework that has been designed earlier in this book (see Figure 6), an inner model can be built easily in SmartPLS by first clicking on the modeling window on the right-hand side, and then selecting the 2nd last blue-color circle icon titled "Switch to Insertion Mode". Click in the window to create those red-color circles that represent your latent variables. Once the circles are placed, right click on each latent variable to change the default name into the appropriate variable name in your model. Press the last icon titled "Switch to Connection Mode" to draw the arrows to connect the variables together (see Figure 12).

Figure 12: Building the Inner Model

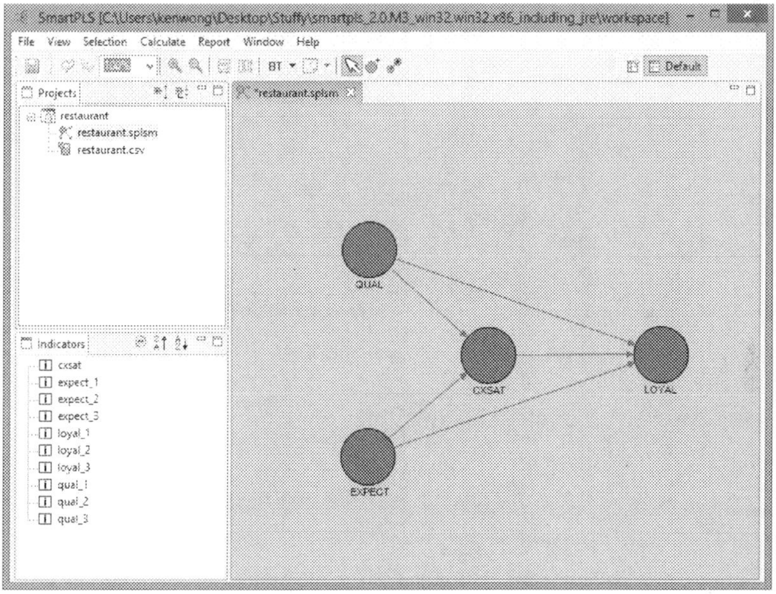

Building the Outer Model

The next step is to build the outer model. To do this, link the indicators to the latent variable by dragging them one-by-one from the "Indicators" tab to the corresponding red circle. Each indicator is represented by a yellow rectangle, and the color of the latent variable will change from red to blue when the linkage is established. The indicators can be easily relocated on the screen by using the "Align Top/Bottom/Left/Right" function, if you right click on the blue-color latent variable. The resulting model should look like those in Figure 13.

Figure 13: Building the Outer Model

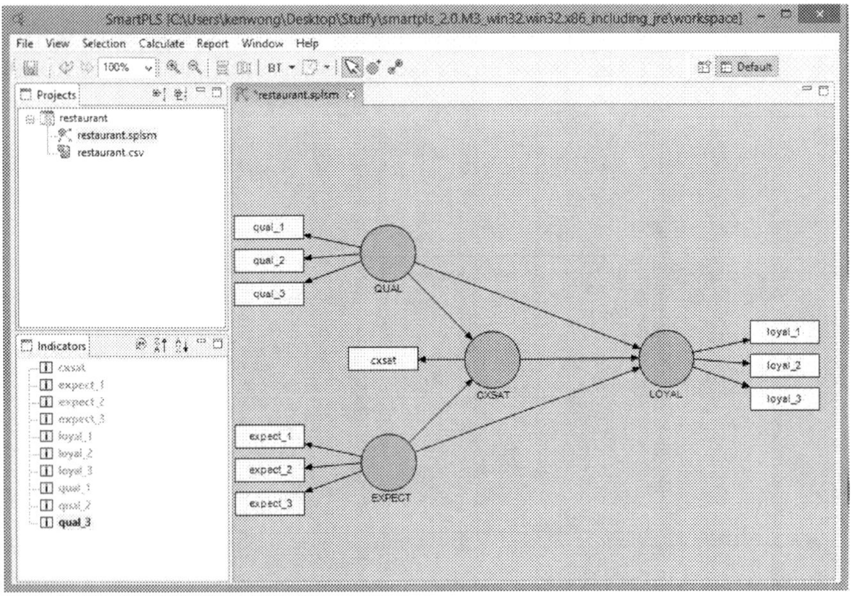

Running the Path-Modeling Estimation

Once the indicators and latent variables are linked together successfully in SmartPLS (i.e., no more red-color circles and arrows), the path modeling procedure can be carried out by going to the "Calculate" menu and selecting "PLS Algorithm"[28]. If the menu is dimmed, just click on the main modeling window to activate it. A pop-up window will be displayed to show the default settings. Since there is no missing value[29] for our data

---

[28] In SmartPLS v2, only the traditional PLS Algorithm is available. In SmartPLS v3, the "Consistent PLS Algorithm (PLSc)" is added to better handle models with "Reflective" constructs. See Chapter 12 for a detailed discussion on this topic.

[29] If there is a missing value in your dataset, choose "Mean Value Replacement" rather than "Case Wise Deletion", as it is the recommended option for PLS-SEM.

set, we proceed directly to the bottom half of the pop-up window to configure the "PLS Algorithm – Settings" with the following parameters (see Figure 14):

- Weighting Scheme: Path Weighting Scheme
- Data Metric: Mean 0, Variance 1
- Maximum Iterations: 300
- Abort Criterion: 1.0E-5
- Initial Weights: 1.0

Figure 14: Configuring the PLS Algorithm

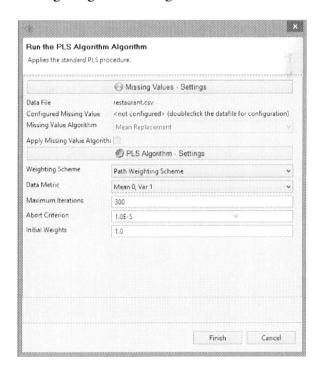

To run the path modeling, press the "Finish" button. There should be no error messages[30] popping up on the screen, and the result can now be assessed and reported.

---

[30] If your data set has an indicator that includes too many identical values, the variance will become zero and lead to a "singular data matrix" error. To fix it, simply remove that indicator from your model.

CHAPTER 4

Evaluating PLS-SEM Results in SmartPLS

The Colorful PLS-SEM Estimations Diagram

SmartPLS presents path modeling estimations not only in the Modeling Window but also in a text-based report[31] which is accessible via the "Report" menu. In the PLS-SEM diagram, there are two types of numbers:

1. Numbers in the circle: These show how much the variance of the latent variable is being explained by the other latent variables.
2. Numbers on the arrow: These are called the path coefficients. They explain how strong the effect of one variable is on another variable. The weight of different path coefficients enables us to rank their relative statistical importance.[32]

The PLS path modeling estimation for our restaurant example is shown in Figure 15.

---

[31] Default Report is the preferred one. You can also choose HTML Report or LaTex Report depending on your needs.

[32] In general, for data set that has up to 1000 observations or samples, the "standardized" path coefficient should be larger than 0.20 in order to demonstrate its significance. Also note that the relative statistical importance of a variable is not the same as its strategic or operational importance.

Figure 15: PLS-SEM Results

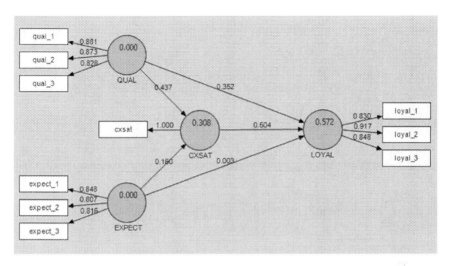

Among all estimation results, the 3 key information that SmartPLS can inform you about the model are:

1. Outer loadings (in reflective measurement model) or outer weights (in formative measurement model)
2. Path coefficients for the structural model relationship
3. R^2 values of the latent endogenous variables

We will first explore these estimations results for model with reflective measurement scale in this Chapter 4, and then those with formative measurement scale in Chapter 5.

Initial Assessment Checklist

Model with Reflective Measurement

For an initial assessment of PLS-SEM, some basic elements should be covered in your research report. If a reflective measurement scale is used, as in our restaurant example, the following topics have to be discussed:

- Explanation of target endogenous variable variance
- Inner model path coefficient sizes and significance

- Outer model loadings and significance
- Indicator reliability*
- Internal consistency reliability*
- Convergent validity[33]
- Discriminant validity*
- Checking Structural Path Significance in Bootstrapping
- Multicollinearity Assessment
- Model's f^2 Effect Size
- Predictive Relevance: The Stone-Geisser's (Q^2) Values
- Total Effect Value

Note: Indicator reliability, internal consistency reliability, and discriminant validity are only applicable to model having a reflective measurement scale.

Model with Formative Measurement

On the other hand, if the model uses a formative measurement scale, the following should be reported instead:

- Explanation of target endogenous variable variance
- Inner model path coefficient sizes and significance
- Outer model weight and significance
- Convergent validity
- Collinearity among indicators
- Checking Structural Path Significance in Bootstrapping
- Multicollinearity Assessment
- Model's f^2 Effect Size
- Predictive Relevance: The Stone-Geisser's (Q^2) Values
- Total Effect Value

We will discuss model that utilizes formative measurement scale in greater details in the next chapter.

---

[33] Note that convergent validity and discriminant validity are measures of construct validity. They do not negate the need for considered selection of measures for proper content and face validity.

Evaluating PLS-SEM Model with Reflective Measurement

By looking at the PLS-SEM estimation diagram in Figure 15, we can make the following preliminary observations:

Explanation of Target Endogenous Variable Variance

- The coefficient of determination, R^2, is 0.572 for the LOYAL endogenous latent variable. This means that the three latent variables (QUAL, EXPECT, and CXSAT) moderately[34] explain 57.2% of the variance in LOYAL.
- QUAL and EXPECT together explain 30.8% of the variance of CXSAT.[35]

Inner Model Path Coefficient Sizes and Significance

- The inner model suggests that CXSAT has the strongest effect on LOYAL (0.504), followed by QUAL (0.352) and EXPECT (0.003).
- The hypothesized path relationship between QUAL and LOYAL is statistically significant.
- The hypothesized path relationship between CXSAT and LOYAL is statistically significant.
- However, the hypothesized path relationship between EXPECT and LOYAL is not statistically significant[36]. This is because its standardized path coefficient (0.003) is lower than 0.1. Thus, we can conclude that: ***CXSAT and QUAL are both moderately strong predictors of LOYAL, but EXPECT does not predict LOYAL directly.***

---

[34] In marketing research, R^2 of 0.75 is substantial, 0.50 is moderate, and 0.25 is weak.

[35] CXSAT acts as both independent and dependent variable in this example and is placed in the middle of the model. It is considered to be an endogenous variable as it has arrows pointing from other latent variables (QUAL and EXPECT) to it. As a rule of thumb, exogenous variable only has arrows pointing away from it.

[36] In SmartPLS, the bootstrap procedure can be used to test the significance of a structural path using T-Statistic.

Outer Model Loadings and Significance

To view the correlations between the latent variable and the indicators in its outer model, go to "Report" in the menu and choose "Default Report". Since we have a reflective model in this restaurant example, we look at the numbers as shown in the "Outer Loadings"[37] window (PLS→ Calculation Results → Outer Loadings). We can press the "Toggle Zero Values" icon to remove the extra zeros in the table for easier viewing of the path coefficients (see Figure 16).

Figure 16: Path Coefficient Estimation in the Outer Model

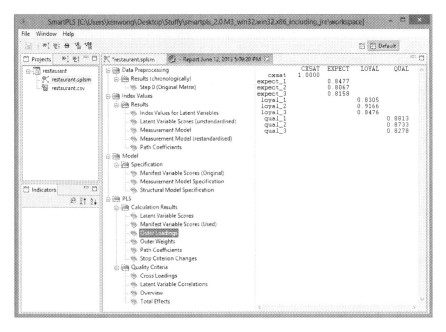

In SmartPLS, the software will stop the estimation when (i) the stop criterion of the algorithm was reached, or (ii) the maximum number of iterations has reached, whichever comes first. Since we intend to obtain a stable estimation, we want the algorithm to converge before reaching the maximum number of iterations. To see if that is the case, go to "Stop Criterion Changes" (see Figure 17) to determine how many iterations have

---

[37] If a "formative" measurement model is used, view "Outer Weights" instead.

been carried out. In this restaurant example, the algorithm converged only after 4 iterations (instead of reaching 300), so our estimation is good[38].

Figure 17: Stop Criterion Changes Table

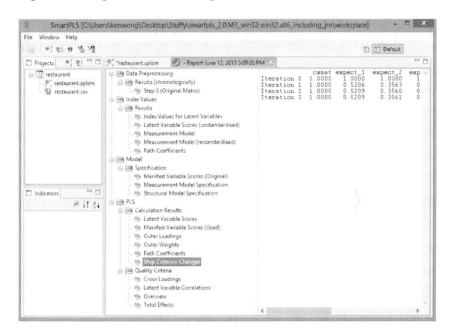

Indicator Reliability[39]

Just like all other marketing research, it is essential to establish the reliability and validity of the latent variables to complete the examination of the measurement model. The following table shows the various reliability and validity items that we must check and report when conducting a PLS-SEM (see Figure 18).

---

[38] If the PLS-SEM algorithm cannot converge your data in less than 300 iterations, it means that your data is abnormal (e.g., sample size too small, existence of outliers, too many identical values in indicator) and requires further investigation.

[39] Do not report indicator reliability if a "formative" measurement is used.

Figure 18: Checking Reliability and Validity

What to check?	What to look for in SmartPLS?	Where is it in the report?	Is it OK?
		Reliability	
Indicator Reliability	"Outer loadings" numbers	PLS→Calculation Results →Outer Loadings	Square each of the outer loadings to find the indicator reliability value. **0.70 or higher** is preferred. If it is an exploratory research, 0.4 or higher is acceptable. (Hulland, 1999)
Internal Consistency Reliability	"Reliability" numbers	PLS→Quality Criteria →Overview	Composite reliability should be **0.7 or higher**. If it is an exploratory research, 0.6 or higher is acceptable. (Bagozzi and Yi, 1988)
		Validity	
Convergent validity	"AVE" numbers	PLS→Quality Criteria →Overview	It should be **0.5 or higher** (Bagozzi and Yi, 1988)
Discriminant validity	"AVE" numbers and Latent Variable Correlations	PLS→Quality Criteria →Overview (for the AVE number as shown above) PLS→Quality Criteria →Latent Variable Correlations	Fornell and Larcker (1981) suggest that the "**square root**" of AVE of each latent variable should be greater than the correlations among the latent variables

To report these reliability and validity figures, tables are often used for reporting purpose (see Figure 19).

Figure 19: Results Summary for Reflective Outer Models

Latent Variable	Indicators	Loadings	Indicator Reliability (i.e., loadings^2)	Composite Reliability	AVE
QUAL	qual_1	0.881	0.777	0.8958	0.7415
	qual_2	0.873	0.763		
	qual_3	0.828	0.685		
EXPECT	expect_1	0.848	0.719	0.8634	0.6783
	expect_2	0.807	0.650		
	expect_3	0.816	0.666		
LOYAL	loyal_1	0.831	0.690	0.8995	0.7494
	loyal_2	0.917	0.840		
	loyal_3	0.848	0.718		

The first one to check is "Indicator Reliability" (see Figure 19). It can be seen that all of the indicators have individual indicator reliability values that are much larger than the minimum acceptable level of 0.4 and close to the preferred level of 0.7.

Internal Consistency Reliability[40]

Traditionally, "Cronbach's alpha" is used to measure internal consistency reliability in social science research but it tends to provide a conservative measurement in PLS-SEM. Prior literature has suggested the use of "Composite Reliability" as a replacement (Bagozzi and Yi, 1988; Hair et al., 2012). From Figure 19, such values are shown to be larger than 0.6, so high levels of internal consistency reliability have been demonstrated among all three reflective latent variables.

That said, the modern view of PLS suggests that instead of using Cronbach's alpha and composite reliability, one should consider using "rho_A" coefficient to check the reliability of PLS construct scores, as defined in Dijkstra and Henseler (2015a). In SmartPLS v3, the "rho_A" value can be found in the Results Report (Quality Criteria → Construct Reliability and Validity) once the PLS or PLSc Algorithm is performed. Generally speaking, a "rho_A" value of 0.7 or larger is preferred to demonstrate composite reliability. Meanwhile, a "rho_A" value above 1 is abnormal and should not occur in the model.

Convergent Validity

To check convergent validity, each latent variable's Average Variance Extracted (AVE) is evaluated. Again from Figure 19, it is found that all of the AVE values are greater than the acceptable threshold of 0.5, so convergent validity is confirmed.

Discriminant Validity[41]

There are two ways to check discriminant validity: the Fornell-Larcker Criterion and HTMT. The classical approach is proposed by Fornell and Larcker (1981) who suggest that the square root of AVE in each latent variable can be used to establish discriminant validity, if this value is larger than other correlation values among the latent variables. To do this, a table is created in which the square root of AVE is manually calculated and

---

[40] Do not report internal consistency reliability if a "formative" measurement is used.

[41] Do not report indicator reliability if a "formative" measurement is used.

written in bold on the diagonal of the table. The correlations between the latent variables are copied from the "Latent Variable Correlation" section of the default report and are placed in the lower left triangle of the table (see Figure 20).

Figure 20: Fornell-Larcker Criterion Analysis for Checking Discriminant Validity

	QUAL	EXPECT	CXSAT	LOYAL
QUAL	**0.861**			
EXPECT	0.655	**0.824**		
CXSAT	0.542	0.446	**Single item construct**	
LOYAL	0.626	0.458	0.695	**0.866**

For example, the latent variable EXPECT's AVE is found to be 0.6783 (from Figure 19) hence its square root becomes 0.824 (see Figure 20). This number is larger than the correlation values in the column of EXPECT (0.446 and 0.458) and also larger than those in the row of EXPECT (0.655). Similar observation is also made for the latent variables QUAL, CXSAT and LOYAL. The result indicates that discriminant validity is well established.

The modern approach to check discriminant validity is to use Heterotrait-monotrait ratio of correlations (HTMT) that is proposed by Henseler, Ringle and Sarstedt (2015). This procedure can be performed in SmartPLS v3 easily and the step-by-step procedure is shown in Chapter 12.

Checking Structural Path Significance in Bootstrapping

SmartPLS can generate T-statistics for significance testing of both the inner and outer model, using a procedure called bootstrapping. In this procedure, a large number of subsamples (e.g., 5000) are taken from the original sample with replacement to give bootstrap standard errors, which in turn gives approximate T-values for significance testing of the structural path. The Bootstrap result approximates the normality of data.

To do this, go to the "Calculate" menu and select "Bootstrapping". In SmartPLS, sample size is known as Cases within the Bootstrapping context, whereas the number of bootstrap subsamples is known as Samples. Since there are 400 valid observations[42] in our restaurant data set, the number of "Cases" (not "Samples") in the setting should be increased to 400 as shown in Figure 21. The other parameters remain unchanged:

1. Sign Change: No Sign Changes
2. Cases: 400
3. Samples: 5000

It worth noting that if the bootstrapping result turns out to be insignificant using the "No Sign Changes" option, but opposite result is achieved using the "Individual Sign Changes" option, you should subsequently re-run the procedure using the middle "Construct Level Changes" option and use that result instead. This is because this option is known to be a good compromise between the two extreme sign change settings.

Figure 21: Bootstrapping Algorithm

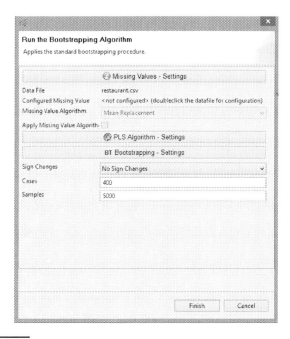

_____

[42] If you have missing data, select "Casewise Replacement" in the Missing Value Algorithm setting. Do not try to use "Mean Replacement" because Bootstrapping draws samples with replacement.

Once the bootstrapping procedure is completed, go to the "Path Coefficients (Mean, STDEV, *T*-Values) window located within the Bootstrapping section of the Default Report. Check the numbers in the "*T*-Statistics" column to see if the path coefficients of the inner model are significant or not. Using a two-tailed *t*-test with a significance level of 5%, the path coefficient will be significant if the *T*-statistics[43] is larger than 1.96. In our restaurant example, it can be seen that only the "EXPECT – LOYAL" linkage (0.0481) is not significant. This confirms our earlier findings when looking at the PLS-SEM results visually (see Figure 15). All other path coefficients in the inner model are statistically significant (see Figure 22 and 23)

Figure 22: Bootstrapping Results-Path Coefficients for Inner Model

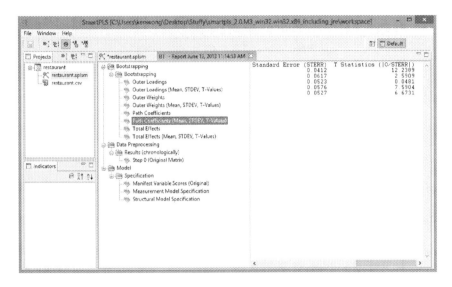

---

[43] The critical *t*-value is 1.65 for a significance level of 10%, and 2.58 for a significance level of 1% (all two-tailed)

Figure 23: *T*-Statistics of Path Coefficients (Inner Model)

	T-Statistics
CXSAT → LOYAL	12.2389
EXPECT → CXSAT	2.5909
EXPECT → LOYAL	0.0481
QUAL → CXSAT	7.5904
QUAL → LOYAL	6.6731

After reviewing the path coefficient for the inner model, we can explore the outer model by checking the *T*-statistic in the "Outer Loadings (Means, STDEV, *T*-Values)" window. As presented in Figure 24, all of the *T*-Statistics are larger than 1.96 so we can say that the outer model loadings are highly significant. All of these results complete a basic analysis of PLS-SEM in our restaurant example.

Figure 24: *T*-Statistics of Outer Loadings

	QUAL	EXPECT	CXSAT	LOYAL
qual_1	57.5315			
qual_2	55.2478			
qual_3	37.0593			
expect_1		42.7139		
expect_2		32.4697		
expect_3		28.9727		
cxsat			Single item construct	
loyal_1				36.3623
loyal_2				97.6560
loyal_3				39.1145

Multicollinearity Assessment

The depth of the PLS-SEM analysis depends on the scope of the research project, the complexity of the model, and common presentation in prior literature. For example, a detailed PLS-SEM analysis would often include a multicollinearity assessment. That is, each set of exogenous latent variables in the inner model[44] is checked for potential collinearity problem to see if any variables should be eliminated, merged into one, or simply have a higher-order latent variable developed.

To assess collinearity issues of the inner model, the latent variable scores (PLS → Calculation Results → Latent Variable Scores) can be used as input for multiple regression in IBM SPSS Statistics to get the tolerance or Variance Inflation Factor (VIF) values, as SmartPLS does not provide these numbers. First, make sure the data set is in .csv file format. Then, import the data into SPSS and go to Analyze → Regression → Linear. In the linear regression module of SPSS, the exogenous latent variables (the predictors) are configured as independent variables, whereas another latent variable (which does not act as a predictor) is configured as the dependent variable. VIF is calculated as "1/Tolerance". As a rule of thumb, we need to have a VIF of 5 or lower (i.e., Tolerance level of 0.2 or higher) to avoid the collinearity problem (Hair et al., 2011).

Model's f^2 Effect Size

In addition to checking collinearity, there can be a detailed discussion of the model's f^2 effect size[45] which shows how much an exogenous latent variable contributes to an endogenous latent variable's R^2 value. In simple terms, effect size assesses the magnitude or strength of relationship between the latent variables. Such discussion can be important because effect size helps researchers to assess the overall contribution of a research study. Chin, Marcolin, and Newsted (1996) have clearly pointed out that researcher should not only indicate whether the relationship between variables is significant or not, but also report the effect size between these variables.

---

[44] Also see the collinearity discussion for formative measurement model in this book for an example.

[45] Effect size of 0.02, 0.15, and 0.35 indicates small, medium, and large effect, respectively.

Predictive Relevance: The Stone-Geisser's (Q^2) Values

Meanwhile, predictive relevance is another aspect that can be explored for the inner model. The Stone-Geisser's (Q^2) values[46] (i.e., cross-validated redundancy measures) can be obtained by the Bindfolding procedure in SmartPLS (Calculate → Bindfolding). In the Bindfolding setting window, an omission distance (OD) of 5 to 10 is suggested for most research (Hair et al., 2012). The q^2 effect size for the Q^2 values can also be computed and discussed.

Total Effect Value

If a mediating latent variable exists in the model, one can also discuss the Total Effect of a particular exogenous latent variable on the endogenous latent variable. Total Effect value can be found in the default report (PLS → Quality Criteria → Total Effects). The significance of Total Effect can be tested using the *T*-Statistics in the Bootstrapping procedure (Bootstrapping → Total Effects (Mean, STDEV, *T*-Values)). Also, unobserved heterogeneity may have to be assessed when there is little information about the underlying data, as it may affect the validity of PLS-SEM estimation. See Chapter 8 for a detailed discussion on the issue of heterogeneity.

Managerial Implications - Restaurant Example

The purpose of this example is to demonstrate how a restaurant manager can improve his/her business by understanding the relationships among customer expectation (EXPECT), perceived quality (QUAL), customer satisfaction (SAT) and customer loyalty (LOYAL). Through a survey of the restaurant patrons and the subsequent structural equation modeling in SmartPLS, the important factors that lead to customer loyalty are identified.

---

[46] Q^2 values of 0.02, 0.15 and 0.35 indicate an exogenous construct has a small, medium and large predictive relevance for an endogenous latent variable respectively.

In this research, customers are found to care about food taste, table service, and bill accuracy. With loadings of 0.881, 0.873 and 0.828 respectively, they are good indicators of perceived quality (QUAL). Restaurant management should not overlook these basic elements of day-to-day operation because perceived quality has been shown to significantly influence customers' satisfaction level, their intention to come back, and whether or not they would recommend this restaurant to others.

Meanwhile, it is also revealed that menu selection, atmospheric elements and good-looking staff are important indicators of customer expectation (EXPECT), with loadings of 0.848, 0.807, and 0.816 respectively. Although fulfilling these customer expectations can keep them satisfied, improvement in these areas does not significantly impact customer loyalty due to its weak effect (0.03) in the linkage. As a result, management should only allocate resources to improve these areas after food taste, table service and bill accuracy have been looked after.

The analysis of inner model shows that perceived quality (QUAL) and customer expectation (EXPECT) together can only explain 30.8% of the variance in customer satisfaction (CXSAT). It is an important finding because it suggests that there are other factors that restaurant managers should consider when exploring customer satisfaction in future research.

CHAPTER 5

Evaluating Model with Formative Measurement

Different Things to Check and Report

As described earlier in this book, a model does not necessarily have reflective measurements. When working with model that utilizes a formative measurement scale, we do not analyze indicator reliability, internal consistency reliability, or discriminant validity because the formative indicators are not highly correlated together. Instead, we analyze the model's outer weight, convergent validity, and collinearity of indicators. In terms of the inner "structural" model, we should check and report the same items as shown in previous chapter. To recap, the followings should be reported if you have a formative measurement model:

- Explanation of target endogenous variable variance
- Inner model path coefficient sizes and significance
- Outer model weight and significance
- Convergent validity
- Collinearity among indicators
- Checking Structural Path Significance in Bootstrapping
- Multicollinearity Assessment
- Model's f^2 Effect Size
- Predictive Relevance: The Stone-Geisser's (Q^2) Values
- Total Effect Value

Outer Model Weight and Significance

For models with formative measurement scale, the outer weights can be found using the path (PLS → Calculation Results → Outer Weight) after the PLS algorithm is run. Marketers should pay attention to those indicators with high outer weights as they are the important area or aspect of the business that should be focused on.

In SmartPLS, bootstrapping can also be used to test the significance of formative indicators' outer weight. After running the procedure, check the *T*-Statistics value as shown in the "Outer Weights" window (Bootstrapping → Bootstrapping → Outer Weights [Mean, STDEV, *T*-Values]). If a particular indicator's outer weight is shown as not significant (i.e., <1.96), check the significance of its outer loading. Only remove the indicator if both of its outer weights and outer loadings are not significant.

Convergent Validity

To establish convergent validity, a "redundancy analysis" can be carried out for each latent variable separately. This involves the use of an existing formative latent variable as an exogenous latent variable to predict an endogenous latent variable operationalized through one or more reflectively measured indicators (see Figure 25).

Figure 25: Redundancy Analysis for Assessing Convergent Validity

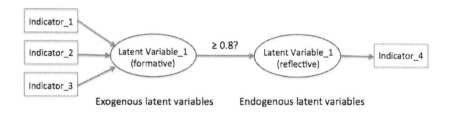

The reflective indicator ("Indicator_4" as in Figure 25) can be a global item in the questionnaire that summarizes the essence of the latent variable the formative indicators ("Indicator_1", "Indicator_2", and "Indicator_3")

intend to measure. For example, if the "Latent Variable_1" is about Corporate Social Responsibility, a survey question such as "Please evaluate to what degree this organization acted in a socially responsible way?" can be asked on a Likert scale of 0 (not a all) to 7 (completely), and this is the data for "Indicator_4".

To do this in SmartPLS, a new model has to be built for each latent variable for PLS-SEM testing. When the correlation (path coefficient) between the latent variables is 0.80 or higher, convergent validity is established (Hair et al., 2013).

Collinearity of Indicators

In a formative measurement model, the problem of indicator collinearity may occur if the indicators are highly correlated to each other. As discussed earlier in the book, multiple regression in SPSS can be used to generate VIF and Tolerance values for collinearity checking. The formative indicators of a latent variable are set as independent variables, with the indicator of another latent variable as dependent variable. In the "Statistics.." window, check "Estimates", "Model Fit" and "Collinearity diagnostics". Once the linear regression is run, locate the "Coefficients" table in the SPSS Output. Only the Tolerance and VIF values showing in the "Collinearity Statistics" column are needed for this collinearity analysis. See Figure 26 for an example.

Figure 26: Tolerance and VIF Values in SPSS Output

Coefficients^a

Model		Unstandardized Coefficients		Standardized Coefficients	t	Sig.	Collinearity Statistics	
		B	Std. Error	Beta			Tolerance	VIF
1	(Constant)	10.387	8.863		1.172	.294		
	indicator_1	-.058	.847	-.040	-.069	.948	.482	2.073
	indicator_2	-.155	.696	-.094	-.223	.833	.922	1.084
	indicator_3	-.228	.577	-.175	-.395	.709	.826	1.211
	indicator_4	-.370	.508	-.384	-.730	.498	.586	1.707

a. Dependent Variable: indicator_8

Looking at a fictitious example as shown in Figure 26, all of the indicators' VIF values are lower than 5 and their Tolerance values are higher than 0.2, so there is no collinearity problem.

Model Having Both Reflective and Formative Measurements

It is important to note that in some research projects, both reflective and formative measurements are present in the same model. In other words, some latent variables have arrows pointing away from them, whereas there are also latent variables that have arrows pointing to them from their indicators. If this is the case, analysis should be carried out separately for each part of the model. Outer loadings and outer weights have to be examined carefully for reflective and formative indicators respectively.

CHAPTER 6

Determining Measurement Model Using Confirmatory Tetrad Analysis (CTA-PLS)

Formative or Reflective? Determining the Measurement Model Quantitatively

Designing the measurement model in PLS-SEM is not always a straight-forward task. It has been a challenge for some researchers to determine if the relationship between the indicators and the latent variable is formative or reflective. This is particularly the case in Marketing when researchers are dealing with innovative products or services where sound theoretical frameworks have not yet been established.

By default, SmartPLS 3 displays a reflective measurement mode for the latent variable. That is, arrows are pointing from the "circular-shaped" latent variable to the "rectangular-shaped" indicators. This can be problematic if the researchers forget to reverse the direction of the arrows when building a formative measurement model. Fortunately, researchers can solve this issue in SmartPLS 3 by making use of a technique called Confirmatory Tetrad Analysis in PLS (CTA-PLS) that is developed by Gudergan, Ringle, Wende, and Will (2008). The only limitation is that CTA-PLS can only check latent variable that has at least 4 indicators associated with it.

The idea behind CTA-PLS is that in a reflective measurement model, each tetrad[47] (τ) is expected to be zero. Hence, if one or more of the tetrads in the measurement model is significantly different from zero, it is formative. In other words, CTA-PLS simply tests the following hypothesis:

$$H_a: \tau \neq 0$$
$$H_0: \tau = 0$$

Case Study: Customer Survey in a Café (B2C)

To illustrate various statistical procedures as presented in Chapter 6, 7 and 8, let us make use of a data set called "cafe100.csv". In this chapter, CTA-PLS will be performed on this data set to check if we should use a reflective, formative, or a combined measurement model.

The data set is a modified version of the one that was originally presented by Wong (2013). A 13-question survey was conducted by a café owner to 100 café patrons to learn about their dining experience so that she can identify and prioritize the key business areas for improvement. Café patrons were asked to rate their experience on a 7-point Likert scales [(1) strongly disagree, (2) disagree, (3) somewhat disagree, (4) neither agree nor disagree, (5) somewhat agree, (6) agree, and (7) strongly agree)] regarding the following 4 major constructs: Customer Expectation (EXPECT), Perceived Quality (QUAL), Customer Satisfaction (CXSAT), and Customer Loyalty (LOYAL). We have also collected data about these café patrons in terms of their customer type (Cxtype; 1 is student, 2 is non-student) and also their loyalty program membership status (member; 1 is member, 2 is non-member). The dataset file is called "cafe100.csv". The indicators and corresponding survey statements are presented in Figure 27:

---

[47] A tetrad is the difference between the product of one pair of covariances and the product of another pair of covariances. By considering the tetrads, researchers can understand the relationship between pairs of covariances.

Figure 27: Indicators and Survey Details

Customer Expectation (EXPECT)	
expect_1	[this cafe] has the best menu selection.
expect_2	[this cafe] has the great atmospheric elements.
expect_3	[this cafe] has good looking servers.
expect_4	[this café] has affordable daily special dishes.
Perceived Quality (QUAL)	
qual_1	The food in [this cafe] is amazing with great taste.
qual_2	Servers in [this cafe] are professional, responsive, and friendly.
qual_3	[this cafe] provides accurate bills to customers.
qual_4	The alcoholic drinks in [this café] are well-crafted.
Customer Satisfaction (CXSAT)	
cxsat	If you consider your overall experiences with [this cafe], how satisfied are you with [this cafe]?
Customer Loyalty (LOYAL)	
loyal_1	I would recommend [this cafe] to my friends and relatives.
loyal_2	I would definitely dine at [this cafe] again in the near future.
loyal_3	If I had to choose again, I would choose [this cafe] as the venue for this dining experience.
loyal_4	I would give high ratings of [this café] on Yelp.

The corresponding theoretical framework is displayed in Figure 28.

Figure 28: Inner Model Design – Café Example.

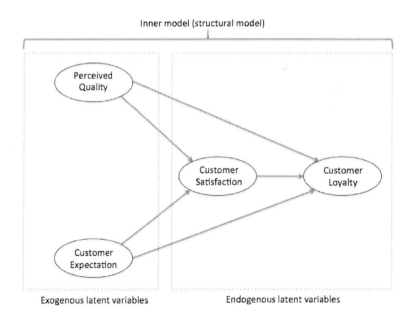

CTA-PLS Procedures

1. Create a new project in SmartPLS using the "cafe100" dataset as in Figure 29.

Figure 29: Model for Cafe100 in SmartPLS

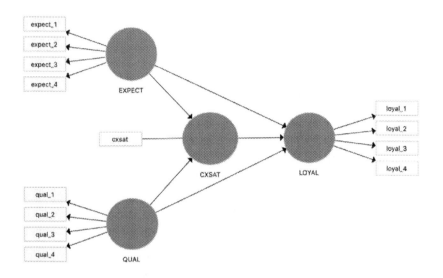

2. Go to the "Calculate" menu and select "PLS Algorithm". Using the following parameters, run the path-modeling estimation by clicking the "Start Calculation" button:

   - Weighting Scheme: Path
   - Maximum Iterations: 500
   - Stop Criterion (10^-X): 7
   - Initial Weights: uncheck the box

3. Look at the bottom of the result page. Under the "Base Data" heading, select "Indicator Data (correlations)" (see Figure 30). Are the numbers mostly different from zero? If Yes, continue to step 4.

Figure 30: Indicator Data (Correlations)

Base Data

Setting

Inner Model

Outer Model

Indicator Data (Original)

Indicator Data (Standardized)

Indicator Data (Correlations)

4. Go back to the "Cafe100.splsm" tab where your colorful model is located. Go to the "Calculate" menu and select "Confirmatory Tetrad Analyses (CTA)". Run the estimation using the following parameters:

    - Subsamples: 5000
    - Do Parallel Processing: checked (ticked)
    - Test Type: Two Tailed
    - Significance level: 0.1

5. Look at the bottom of the result page. Under the "Final Results" heading, click the hyperlink for the variable "EXPECT".
6. Scroll to the right to view the last 2 columns. Check the "CI Low adj." and "CI Up adj." columns to see if zero falls in-between these 2 values. If Yes, it is reflective (See Figure 31).

Figure 31: Confidence Interval Values

Copy to Clipboard:		Excel Format	R Format
Alpha adj.	**z(1-alpha)**	**CI Low adj.**	**CI Up adj.**
0.050	1.960	-0.542	0.242
0.050	1.960	-0.647	0.531

7. In this example, there are two tetrads for the EXPECT variable. Since zero falls into this bias-corrected and Bonferroni-adjusted confidence interval, the tetra is not significantly different from zero, meaning it is having a "reflective" measurement model. As a result, we can safely use the default SmartPLS 3 setting to make the arrows pointing from the circular-shape EXPECT to the rectangular-shaped indicators when designing the model.

8. The following Figure 32 may be used as a guideline to determine if the measurement model is formative or reflective:

Figure 32: Guideline for Using CI to Determine Measurement Model

	CI Low adj.	CI Up adj.		Measurement Model is
If all values are…	-	-	then	formative
If all values are…	+	+	then	formative
If one or more of the values are	-	+	then	reflective

9. Following the same process, we check the other variables LOYAL and QUAL in the result report. It was found that LOYAL and QUAL were both having the reflective measurement model. As such, there is no need to change the arrow directions in our model as SmartPLS uses the reflective measurement model as the default setting.

10. When CTA-PLS cannot be applied, such as having latent variable with 3 or fewer indicators, researchers should then make the formative vs. reflective decision based on sound theoretical considerations. As a rule of thumb, if the indicators hang well together and are highly interchangeable among themselves, it is a reflective measurement model. On the other hand, if the indicators are not highly correlated and they are not interchangeable, a formative measurement model is suggested (Wong, 2013).

CHAPTER 7

Handling Non-Linear Relationship Using Quadratic Effect Modeling (QEM)

Non-linear Relationship Explained

Experienced researchers would agree that variables do not always hold a linear relationship as in a straight line (Hay & Morris, 1991; Eisenbeiss, Cornelißen, Backhaus, & Hoyer, 2014). For example, in the field of marketing, advertising activities and sales revenue often hold a non-linear, quadratic relationship.[48] Consumers may be eager to buy a firm's product or service after watching an attractive advertisement, but their intentions to make such purchases gradually drop after initial excitement is gone, even if they are being exposed to the advertisements continuously. In other words, the effect of advertising on sales gradually diminishes even though they have a positive relationship overall.

The same can be said for the relationship between customer satisfaction and loyalty. Although customer satisfaction (CXSAT) is usually affecting loyalty (LOYAL) in a positive way, they do not necessarily dictate a straight linear relationship all the time. In reality, customer satisfaction and loyalty often hold a non-linear, quadratic relationship. It is not uncommon to see customer's loyalty towards a brand peaked out after a period of time even

---

[48] There are four possible non-linear, quadratic effects that we can model. They are: (i) concave downward with a positive slope, (ii) concave downward with a negative slope, (iii) concave upward with a positive slope, and (iv) concave upward with a negative slope.

when they are still highly satisfied with the product or service. If we draw a graph, this relationship can be represented by a concave downward curve with a positive slope (see Figure 33).

Figure 33: Non-linear Relationship Between Customer Satisfaction and Loyalty

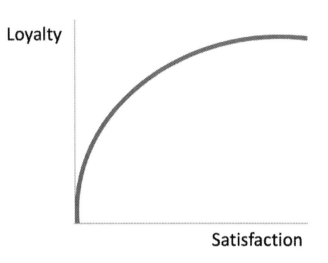

Technically speaking, the non-linear relationship can be viewed as a linear relationship that is moderated by a newly created quadratic term (variable) that is a self-interaction of the exogenous construct (e.g., CXSAT * CXSAT).

To determine whether the variable of interest is having a linear or non-linear relationship, one should assess the following 2 aspects in PLS-SEM:
1. The significance of the quadratic term
2. The f^2 effect size of the quadratic term[49]

QEM Procedures

1. Let us use the "café100" dataset for illustration. Assuming that we suspect a non-linear relationship exists between customer

---

[49] According to Cohen (1988), 0.02, 0.15, and 0.35 represent small, medium and large effect sizes respectively.

satisfaction (CXSAT) and customer loyalty (LOYAL), we can run Quadratic Effect Modeling (QEM) to see if that is the case.

2. First, we need to create a quadratic term in the "Cafe100.splsm" tab. In our colorful model, right-click on the dependent variable (e.g., LOYAL) and choose "Add Quadratic Effect...". (see Figure 34).

Figure 34: Adding Quadratic Effect

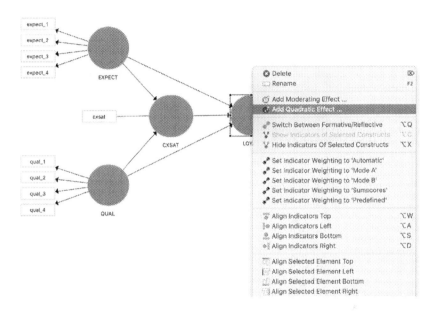

3. Select the independent variable "CXSAT" and set Calculation Method as "Two Stage" (see Figure 35). Use the other default settings. Click the "OK" button to build that Quadratic term.

Figure 35: Quadratic Effect Settings

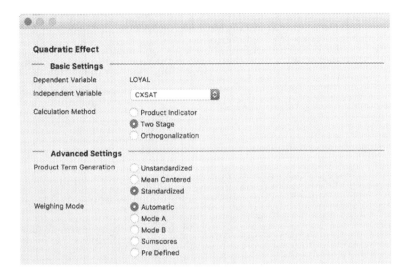

4. Rename the newly created quadratic term from "Quadratic Effect 1" to "CXSATq". Right click on it and select "Show Indicators of Selected Constructs" (see Figure 36).

Figure 36: Renaming the Quadratic Term

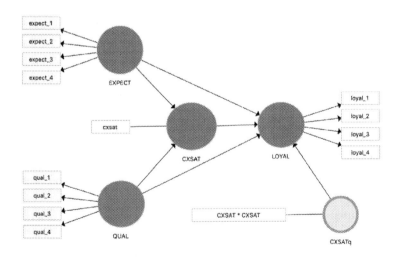

5. Go to the "Calculate" menu and select "PLS Algorithm". Run the estimation to obtain the path coefficients (see Figure 37).

Figure 37: PLS Algorithm Results

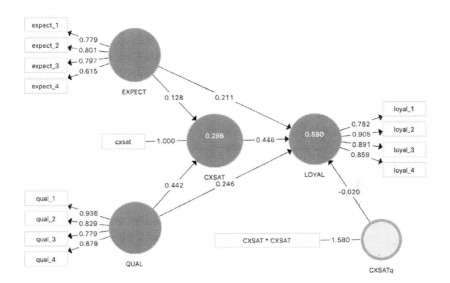

The following equation illustrates the results of the relationship between CXSAT and LOYAL:

$$\text{LOYAL} = 0.446 * \text{CXSAT} - 0.020 * \text{CXSATq}$$

6. The significance of the quadratic term can then be determined using the "Bootstrapping" procedure. Go to the "Calculate" menu to select "Bootstrapping". Run it using a subsample of 5000 (see Figure 38):

Figure 38: Bootstrapping

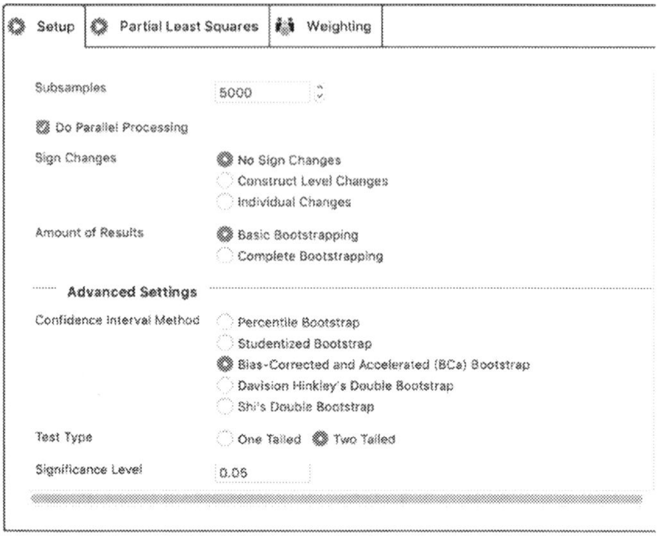

7. Once bootstrapping is completed, look at the "Mean, STDEV, T-Values, P-Value" tab in the Path Coefficients report. Check the corresponding *p*-value using the following hypotheses and a significance level of 0.05 (see Figure 39):

H_A: *Satisfaction and Loyalty have significant non-linear, quadratic effect.*

H_0: *Satisfaction and Loyalty have insignificant non-linear, quadratic effect.*

Figure 39: P-Values for the Quadratic Term Linkage

Path Coefficients

	Mean, STDEV, T-Values, P-Values	Confidence Intervals		Confidence Intervals Bias Correct...

	Original Sample (O	Sample Mean (M)	Standard Deviatior	T Statistics (|O/ST	P Values
CXSAT -> LOYAL	0.446	0.436	0.089	5.008	0.000
CXSATq -> LOYAL	-0.020	-0.027	0.057	0.352	0.725
EXPECT -> CXSAT	0.128	0.142	0.127	1.011	0.312
EXPECT -> LOYAL	0.211	0.216	0.085	2.489	0.013
QUAL_ -> CXSAT	0.442	0.436	0.132	3.339	0.001
QUAL_ -> LOYAL	0.246	0.247	0.089	2.747	0.006

8. From Figure 35, it can be seen that in the CXSATq → LOYAL row, the resulting P-Value is 0.725, which is larger than our significance level of 0.05. As a result, we accept the null hypothesis that Customer Satisfaction (CXSAT) and Loyalty (LOYAL) do not hold any significant non-linear, quadratic effect.

9. To confirm, we can double check the "Confidence Intervals Bias Corrected" tab (see Figure 40):

Figure 40: 95% Bias Corrected Confidence Interval

Path Coefficients

Mean, STDEV, T-Values, P-Values	Confidence Intervals		Confidence Intervals Bias Correct...	
	Original Sample (O	Sample Mean (M)	Bias	2.5%	97.5%
CXSAT -> LOYAL	0.446	0.436	-0.010	0.274	0.619
CXSATq -> LOYAL	-0.020	-0.027	-0.007	-0.127	0.099
EXPECT -> CXSAT	0.128	0.142	0.014	-0.142	0.358
EXPECT -> LOYAL	0.211	0.216	0.004	0.031	0.370
QUAL_ -> CXSAT	0.442	0.436	-0.006	0.184	0.706
QUAL_ -> LOYAL	0.246	0.247	0.002	0.079	0.427

In the CXSATq → LOYAL row, the value zero falls in between the lower bound of -0.127 and upper bound of 0.099. Based on the 95% bias-corrected confidence interval, it can be concluded once again that CXSAT's non-linear, quadratic effect on LOYAL is insignificant.

10. Other than assessing the significance of the quadratic term, one has to evaluate the strength of the nonlinear effect as well, by means of the f^2 effect size of the quadratic term. Go to the "PLS Algorithm (Run No._)" tab and look at the bottom of the page. Under the "Quality Criteria" heading, click the "f Square" hyperlink to view the f^2 effect size (see Figure 41).

Figure 41: Quality Criteria: f^2 Effect Size

f Square

		CXSAT	CXSATq	EXPECT	LOYAL	QUAL_
Matrix	f Square					
CXSAT					0.211	
CXSATq					0.001	
EXPECT		0.013			0.060	
LOYAL						
QUAL_		0.154			0.071	

11. From Figure 41, the quadratic term CXSATq has a f^2 effect size of 0.001, which is smaller than the lower limit of 0.02 as proposed by Cohen (1988). The low f^2 effect size, combined with the non-significance of the quadratic effect, clearly suggests that customer satisfaction and loyalty have a linear relationship in our dataset.

CHAPTER 8

Analysing Segments Using Heterogeneity Modeling

Something is Hiding in the Dataset

In exploratory research, marketing researchers may have little knowledge about the nature of the underlying data. They need to consider the potential problem of heterogeneous data structures in PLS-SEM modeling because the data do not necessarily come from a homogeneous population (see Figure 42).

Figure 42: Mixture Distribution vs. Segment-specific Distributions

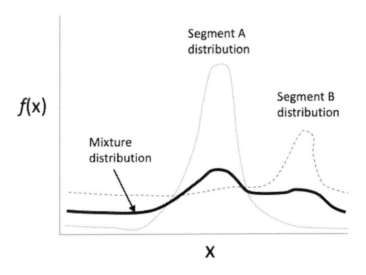

If heterogeneity is established, researchers may need to estimate two or more separate models to avoid drawing an incorrect conclusion about the model relationships (Sarstedt, Schwaiger, & Ringle, 2009). There are two kinds of heterogeneity: observed and unobserved ones. Observed heterogeneity often happens between two or more groups due to the presence of a categorical moderator variable, such as demographic differences (e.g., age, gender, or nationality). On the other hand, unobserved heterogeneity may occur without driven by obvious, observable group characteristics. Researchers need to treat unobserved heterogeneity because it biases parameter estimates, threatens different types of validity[50] due to Type I and Type II errors, and leads to invalid conclusions[51] (Jedidi et al., 1997).

Establishing Measurement Invariance (MICOM)

Before running any multigroup analysis, researchers need to first establish measurement invariance[52] in PLS-SEM in order to eliminate measurement error and protect the validity of the outcomes. This can be achieved by using the "Measurement Invariance of the Composite Models" (MICOM) procedure as proposed by Henseler, Ringle, and Sarstedt (2016). If measurement invariance is not established prior to performing multi-group analysis, the conclusion can be questionable because the model may suffer from low power of statistical tests and low precision of estimators (Hult et al., 2008).

The MICOM procedure consists of 3 steps that should be completed in sequence. The first step is to test "Configural invariance", the second step is to test "Compositional invariance". The third step is to test "composite means and variances". Both the configural invariance and compositional invariance have to be established prior to running any multi-group analysis. If either one is not established, researchers should analyze the groups

---

[50] Types of validity being affected by unobserved heterogeneity include internal validity, instrumental validity, statistical conclusion validity, and external validity.
[51] For example, a researcher may conclude that an independent variable is insignificant in the combined model, when in fact it should be significant due to the effects of this independent variable in each unobserved segment cancel each other. See explanation in Becker et al., (2013).
[52] Measurement invariance is also known as measurement equivalence.

separately and not performing any multi-group analysis. Once these two invariances are both established, the equality of composite means and variances can be checked. If they are equal, full measurement invariance is established. This means that multigroup analysis can be performed and pooling of data is possible. Otherwise, partial measurement invariance is established, meaning multigroup analysis can still be performed but pooling of data is not possible.

A. Modeling Observed Heterogeneous Data

Different kinds of techniques have been proposed to handle *a priori* groupings in multi-group analysis[53] (Keil et al, 2000; Sarstedt and Mooi, 2014; Henseler et al., 2009; Chin and Dibbern, 2010). To compare two groups of data in PLS-SEM specifically[54], the non-parametric "Permutation test" is suggested due to its advantageous statistical properties, such as having no data distributional assumptions and being able to perform well across a broad range of conditions (Ernst, 2004; Good, 2000).

Permutation Test Procedures

1. Let us use the "café100" dataset again for illustration. In this example, the café patrons can be categorized into 2 groups: students (code: 1) and non-students (code: 2).
2. In SmartPLS, under the "Project Explorer" tab in the upper left-hand side of the window, double click the "cafe100 [100 records]" data file which has a green icon.
3. At the top of the window, there is a button called "Generate Data Groups". Click it to create a new grouping variable.

---

[53] These techniques include the Parametric *t*-test (Keil et al., 2000), the Parametric Levene's test (Sarstedt and Mooi, 2014), the non-parametric Partial Least Squares-Multigroup Analysis [PLS-MGA] (Henseler et al., 2009), the non-parametric permutation test (Chin and Dibbern, 2010), and the Omnibus test of group differences [OTG] (Sarstedt, Henseler, and Ringle, 2011).
[54] For comparison among 3 or more groups, the Omnibus Test of Group differences (OTG) procedure is recommended instead. See detailed description from Sarstedt, Henseler, and Ringle (2011).

4. In the "Generate Data Groups" window, click the "Group column 0:" pull-down menu to select "cxtype (2 unique values)" (see Figure 43):

Figure 43: Generating New Grouping Variable

Generate Data Groups

Name prefix:	GROUP_

Group Columns

Group column 0:	cxtype (2 unique values)
Group column 1:	
Group column 2:	

Prune groups

Total:	2
Minimum cases:	10

5. Press OK. You should be able to see the customer distribution information as in Figure 44:

Figure 44: Data Groups

Delimiter:	Comma	Encoding:	UTF-8
Value Quote Character:	None	Sample size:	100
Number Format:	US (e.g. 1,000.23)	Indicators:	15
Missing Value Marker:	None	Missing Values:	3

Indicators:	Indicator Correlations	Raw File	Data Groups	

Name	Records	
GROUP_cxtype(1.0)	44	Delete
GROUP_cxtype(2.0)	56	

6. Go back to the colorful "Cafe100.splsm" model tab. In the "Calculate" menu, select "Permutation". Under the "Setup" tab, click the "Group A" pull-down menu to select "GROUP_cxtype(1.0)". Similarly, click the "Group B" pull-down menu to select "GROUP_cxtype(2.0)" (see Figure 45):

Figure 45: Permutation

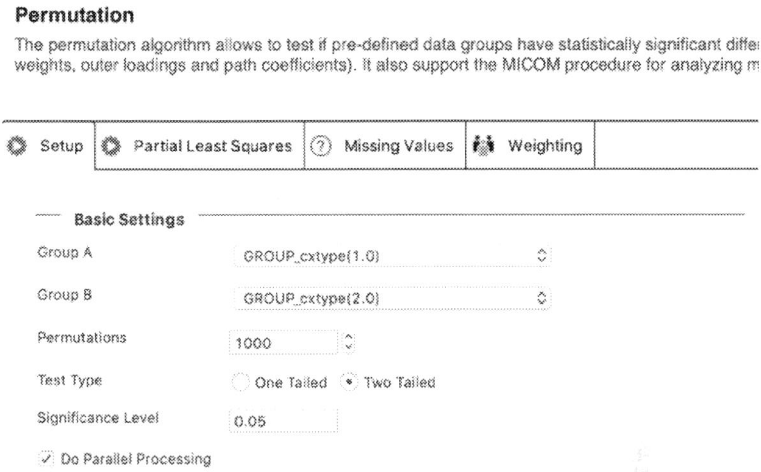

Permutation

The permutation algorithm allows to test if pre-defined data groups have statistically significant differ weights, outer loadings and path coefficients). It also support the MICOM procedure for analyzing m

⚙ Setup	⚙ Partial Least Squares	⊘ Missing Values	👥 Weighting	

— **Basic Settings** ————————————————————

Group A	GROUP_cxtype(1.0) ⌄
Group B	GROUP_cxtype(2.0) ⌄
Permutations	1000 ⌄
Test Type	⚪ One Tailed 🔘 Two Tailed
Significance Level	0.05
☑ Do Parallel Processing	

7. Start calculation using the following parameters:
    - Permutations: 1000
    - Test Type: Two Tailed
    - Significance Level: 0.05
    - Do Parallel Processing: Checked [ticked]
8. To establish "Configural invariance" as in Step 1 of the MICOM procedure, we need to ensure that (i) the PLS path models, (ii) data treatment, and (iii) algorithm settings of both groups are exactly the same. Since this is the case when we perform the permutation model estimation, we have established configural invariance.
9. Next, we want to establish "Compositional invariance" as in Step 2 of the MICOM procedure. To do this, we examine the "Permutation p-Values" of the constructs. Select the MICOM hyperlink under the "Quality Criteria" heading at the bottom of the result page and look at the last column in the "Step 2" tab (see Figure 46).

Figure 46: MICOM

MICOM

Step 2	Step 3			
	Original Correlatio	Correlation Permu	5.0%	Permutation p-Values
CXSAT	1.000	1.000	1.000	0.293
CXSATq	1.000	1.000	1.000	0.068
EXPECT	0.966	0.977	0.929	0.204
LOYAL	0.999	0.999	0.996	0.350
QUAL.	1.000	0.998	0.993	0.906

10. Since all constructs have their "Permutation p-Values" larger than 0.05, we accept the null hypothesis that the original correlations of these constructs are not significantly different from 1. This gives us supporting evidence that compositional invariance has been established in the model.

11. We can proceed to check whether we have achieved full measurement invariance or just partial measurement invariance by looking at the composite means and variances, as in Step 3 of MICOM. This information is presented in the "Step 3" tab (see Figure 47).

Figure 47: Permutation p-Values

MICOM

Step 2	Step 3									
	Mean - Origi	Mean - Permut	2.5%	97.5%	Permutation p-Values	Variance - Origi	Variance - P	2.5%	97.5%	Permutation p-Values
CXSAT	0.348	-0.004	-0.402	0.378	0.085	-0.532	0.010	-0.630	0.667	0.120
CXSATq	-0.476	0.020	-0.572	0.665	0.152	-1.720	0.007	-1.726	1.838	0.059
EXPECT	0.477	0.006	-0.409	0.425	0.019	-0.156	-0.002	-0.487	0.460	0.518
LOYAL	0.407	0.002	-0.400	0.391	0.044	-1.021	-0.011	-0.780	0.694	0.008
QUAL.	0.280	0.005	-0.413	0.422	0.267	-0.406	-0.014	-0.537	0.435	0.105

12. The first few columns show information about the Mean, whereas the last 5 columns show information about the Variance. From Figure 47, it can be seen that not all of the mean's "Permutation p-value" are larger than 0.05. Similarly, in terms of variance, some constructs have their "Permutation p-value" smaller than

0.05, we, therefore, accept the alternative hypothesis that there are significant differences in the composite mean values and variances of latent variables across the two groups. In other words, we can only establish partial measurement invariance because not all the composite mean values and variances are equal.

13. The final step is to explore the path coefficients. Look at the "Final Results" heading and select the "Path Coefficients" hyperlink at the bottom of the result page. Compare the path coefficients of the groups (see first two columns in Figure 48) and also look at their "Permutation p-Values" in the last column.

Figure 48: Path Coefficients

Path Coefficients							
Matrix							Copy to Clipboard
	Path Coefficients Original (GROUP_extype(1.0))	Path Coefficients Original (GROUP_extype(2.0))	Path Coefficients Path Coefficients		2.5%	97.5%	Permutation p-Values
CXSAT -> LOYAL	0.361	0.402	-0.041	-0.092	-0.370	0.338	0.840
CXSAT -> LOYAL	-0.167	0.002	-0.169	-0.006	-0.242	0.228	0.153
EXPECT -> CXSAT	0.143	0.130	0.013	0.001	-0.481	0.485	0.959
EXPECT -> LOYAL	0.422	0.071	0.351	0.008	-0.334	0.340	0.039
QUAL, -> CXSAT	0.147	0.568	-0.421	0.010	-0.500	0.538	0.116
QUAL, -> LOYAL	0.034	0.408	-0.374	-0.005	-0.348	0.370	0.039

14. From Figure 48, it can be seen that the 2 key linkages, "EXPECT → LOYAL" and "QUAL → LOYAL", both have a Permutation p-values of 0.039. This means that effect between EXPECT and LOYAL is significantly ($p \leq 0.05$) different between café patrons who are students ($p^1 = 0.422$) and those who are non-students ($p^2 = 0.071$). Similarly, we can draw the conclusion that effect between QUAL and LOYAL is significantly ($p \leq 0.05$) different between café patrons who are students ($p^1 = 0.034$) and those who are non-students ($p^2 = 0.408$).

15. Reviewing the original survey questions and the above results can help the café manager to draw some managerial implications. We can argue that students care more about the Customer Expectation (EXPECT) than non-students, when it comes to affecting their loyalty intentions. This argument is logical, one of the indicators for the EXPECT construct, expect_4, is related to affordable daily special dishes. If the café owner would like to continue earning

loyalty from the students, it is advisable for the café owner to keep the daily specials and not removing it from the menu.

16. Similarly, the result shows that non-students put a heavier focus on the Perceived Quality (QUAL). This is not surprising as one of the indicators, qual_4, refers to how well the café can craft alcoholic drinks, something that only excites the more matured, non-student café patrons.

B. Modeling Unobserved Heterogeneous Data

When there are suspicious differences in structural path coefficients but the existing theory does not assume heterogeneity, the model may be affected by unobserved heterogeneity. Many tools have been proposed to identify and treat such heterogeneity in PLS-SEM[55], but researchers have recommended the use of "latent class techniques"[56] such as Finite Mixture Partial Least Squares (FIMIX-PLS) (Sarstedt, Becker, Ringle, & Schwaiger, 2011) and PLS Prediction-oriented Segmentation (PLS-POS) (Becker, Rai, Ringle, and Völckner, 2013). These two techniques are handy because FIMIX-PLS is an effective tool to reveal the number of segments hiding in the underlying data, whereas PLS-POS can then be used to explain the structure of latent segment and estimate segment-specific models.

When the PLS path models include formative measures, PLS-POS is preferred over other latent class techniques for checking unobserved heterogeneity in both structural and measurement models. This method manages heterogeneity by using a distance measure that facilitates the reassignment of observations with the objective of improving the prediction-oriented optimization criterion (Becker et al., 2013).

Once FIMIX-PLS and PLS-POS are performed, researchers can carry out ex-post analysis to identify explanatory variables and elaborate on the

---

[55] Examples include distance measure-based methods like PLS-TPM (Squillacciotti 2005) and REBUS-PLS (Esposito Vinzi et al., 2010). However, these methods cannot uncover unobserved heterogeneity in PLS-SEM with formative measures, so their usage is restricted.

[56] Latent class techniques have been used in CB-SEM for decades (Muthén, 1989) but only got popular in PLS-SEM in recent years (Esposito Vinzi, Trinchera, Squillacciotti & Tenehaus, 2008).

theory. By turning unobserved heterogeneity into observed heterogeneity in the dataset, researchers can then test and validate the segment-specific path models. As pointed out by Becker et al. (2013), a well-defined segment should be substantial, differentiable, plausible, and accessible. These are the important checkpoints when we go through the process of modeling unobserved heterogeneous data.

(i) FIMIX-PLS Procedures

1. The first step of FIMIX-PLS is to manage missing data in the dataset. If there are missing values, researchers should delete those observations that have missing values using the casewise deletion method, instead of replacing them with the mean value. To find out if there are any missing values in the dataset, click the green icon of the data file "cafe100 [100 records]" and then look at the "cafe100.txt" tab on the right-hand side of the screen. Go to the "Indicators:" tab and look at the "Missing" column. From the following Figure 49, we can see that there is a total of 3 incomplete observations in our "cafe100" dataset.

Figure 49: Fixing missing data using casewise deletion.

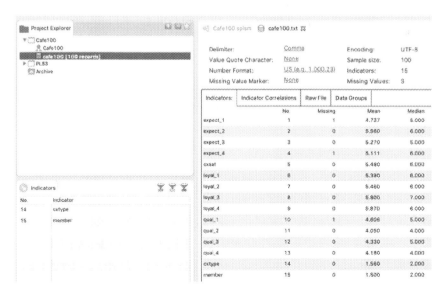

2. There are some missing values in the indicators expect_1, expect_4, and qual_1. To address this problem, first click the colorful "Cafe100.splsm" tab. Go to the "Calculate" menu and select "Finite Mixture (FIMIX) Segmentation". Then, view the "Missing Values" tab and select "Casewise Deletion" (see Figure 50). Note that if there are no missing values in the dataset, this "Missing Values" tab will not be shown at all in FIMIX.

Figure 50: Casewise Deletion in FIMIX

3. Since we are exploring unobserved heterogeneous data, we do not know precisely how many relevant segments (or groups) there are in the dataset a priori. Although we can use a common approach to determine the potential number of segments such as dividing the number of observations by the minimum sample size[57], we can also make an educated guess by considering the model background, the data distributional characteristics, and the variables' psychometric properties. As we have a small dataset with only 97 observations after casewise deletion, we tentatively suggest the potential presence of 4 customer segments to begin the FIMIX-PLS procedure and let the results confirm this number.

4. Create a table like the following one to show the index fit:

---

[57] For minimum sample size requirement, see Marcoulides & Saunders (2006) and Wong (2013).

Figure 51: Number of Segments

	# of segments			
Information Criteria[16]	1	2	3	4
AIC				
AIC$_3$				
AIC$_4$				
BIC				
CAIC				
MDL$_5$				
LnL				

(Note: For the fit measure in each information criterion, the optimal solution is the number of segments with the lowest value. The only exception is LnL (LogLikeihood) where the bigger the value, the better it is.)

5. Go back to the "Setup" tab to perform FIMIX-PLS calculation using the following parameters:
   - Number of Segments: 1 [Yes, select 1 and not 2 here to create our initial estimation]
   - Maximum number of iterations: 5000
   - Stop Criterion: 5 (→1.0E-5) [If you see a red icon there, just click the arrow up and then down]
   - Number of Repetitions: 10

6. On the FIMIX result page, first check the fit indices by going to the "Quality Criterion" heading and clicking the "Fit indices" hyperlink for a model with only one segment. Copy the data (see Figure 52) and paste them into the table created in step 4.

Figure 52: Fit Indices

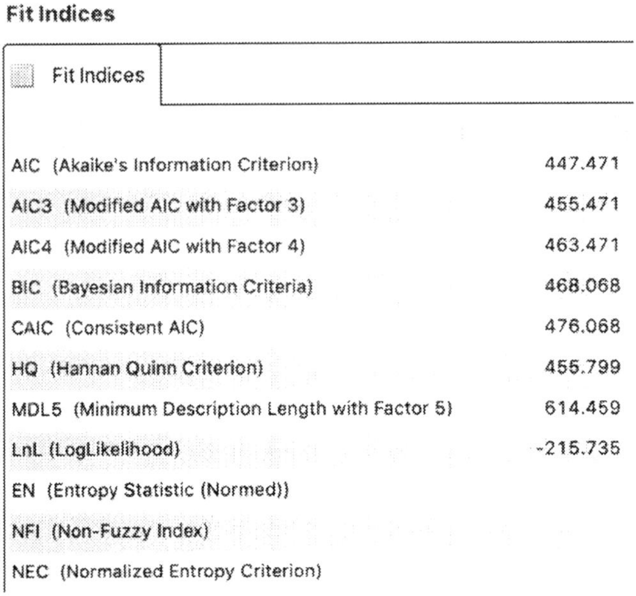

Fit Indices

Fit Indices	
AIC (Akaike's Information Criterion)	447.471
AIC3 (Modified AIC with Factor 3)	455.471
AIC4 (Modified AIC with Factor 4)	463.471
BIC (Bayesian Information Criteria)	468.068
CAIC (Consistent AIC)	476.068
HQ (Hannan Quinn Criterion)	455.799
MDL5 (Minimum Description Length with Factor 5)	614.459
LnL (LogLikelihood)	-215.735
EN (Entropy Statistic (Normed))	
NFI (Non-Fuzzy Index)	
NEC (Normalized Entropy Criterion)	

7. Since we made an educated guess about having 4 segments in the dataset, re-run the FIMIX-PLS calculation using the following parameters in the "Setup" tab:
   - Number of Segments: 4
   - Maximum number of iterations: 5000
   - Stop Criterion: 5 (→1.0E-5) [If you see a red icon there, just click the arrow up and then down]
   - Number of Repetitions: 10

8. Check the fit indices once again by going to the "Quality Criterion" heading and selecting "Fit indices" for a model with two segments. Copy the data and paste them into the table. Following this logic, if you have 5 potential segments in your dataset, for example, you have to create a table with 5 columns for the segments and then run the FIMIX-PLS procedure 5 times (i.e., first time with 1 segment, second time with 2 segments, third time with 3 segments…etc.) using different number of segments to find out their corresponding Fit Indices.

9. In each row, we bold the optimal fit index value. For example, in the AIC row, we bold the value 393.802 as it is the lowest value, whereas in the LnL row, we bold the-161.901 as it is the highest value. From Table 4, we can see that the 1-segment model has 3 optimal solutions (i.e., only BIC, CAIC, and MDL_5 are in bold), the 2-segment model has no optimal solution, the 3-segment solution has just 1 optimal solution (i.e., AIC_4 is in bold), whereas the 4-segment model has the most number of optimal solutions (i.e., AIC, AIC_3, HQ and LnL are in bold). This leads us to believe that the dataset has 4 underlying segments technically speaking.

Figure 53: Fit Indices Based on Number of Segments

Information Criteria[17]	# of segments			
	1	2	3	4
AIC	447.471	430.314	407.270	**393.802**
AIC_3	455.471	447.314	433.270	**428.802**
AIC_4	463.471	464.314	**459.270**	463.802
BIC	**468.068**	474.084	474.213	483.917
CAIC	**476.068**	491.084	500.213	518.917
HQ	455.799	448.013	434.338	**430.240**
MDL_5	**614.459**	785.165	949.982	1224.376
LnL	-215.735	-198.157	-177.635	**-161.901**

(note: optimal value in bold)

10. As discussed earlier, the segments should be **substantial** in size to represent a "real" segment. Researcher needs to eliminate the small segments[58] that are irrelevant for theory or practice. We can also look at their sample sizes by going to the Result report and clicking the "Segment Sizes" hyperlink under the "Final Results" heading. From Figure 54, it can be seen that Segment 1 is 39.4% of the data, Segment 2 is 27.2% of the data, Segment 3 is 19.8% of the data, whereas Segment 4 is the smallest one that makes up 13.7% of the data. These segments are big enough in general for

---

[58] Small segments may be caused by outliers, data collection problems, or other statistical artifacts.

our modeling. In case the resulting segment(s) are tiny (e.g., 2%), marketing researcher should consider eliminating them from the investigation as they are not substantial.

Figure 54: Segment Sizes

Segment Sizes

Matrix	Copy to Clipboard:	Excel Format	R Format
	Segment 1	Segment 2	Segment 3	Segment 4
%	0.394	0.272	0.198	0.137

11. Using FIMIX-PLS, we conclude that there are 4 segments in our "cafe100" dataset.

12. The next step is to better understand the data in each of these identified segments. The FIMIX-PLS technique that we have just performed is limited to uncovering unobserved heterogeneity in the structural model only, it cannot handle model with formative measures properly. Meanwhile, the other statistical procedure, PLS-POS, can reveal unobserved heterogeneity in both the measurement and structural models. As such, PLS-POS is highly recommended for exploring the identified segments further, such as calculating the average explained variance R^2 and path coefficients. In other words, we should use FIMIX-PLS only to identify the number of segments presented in the dataset and then use PLS-POS to explore the remaining properties of the model.

(ii) PLS-POS Procedures

1. Click the colorful "Cafe100.splsm" model tab. Go to the "Calculate" menu and select "Prediction-Orientation Segmentation (POS)". In the "Setup" tab, start calculation use the following parameters:
   - Groups: 4 [based on our FIMIX-PLS result where it identified 4 segments]

- Maximum Iterations: 1000 [Multiply our number of observations by 2 and compare that to the default value of 1000. Then, select the higher of the two]
- Search Depth: 100 [this should equal the number of observations, which is 100.]
- Initial Separation: FIMIX Segmentation
- Pre-segmentation: [uncheck]
- Optimization Criterion: Sum of all Construct Weighted R-Squares

2. In case you see a red-color icon next to the grey-out "Start Calculation" button, go to the "Finite Mixture (FIMIX) Segmentation" tab, click the arrow up and down in the "Stop Criterion" line to make it read 5, then go back to the "Setup" page to run the algorithm.

3. Run the PLS-POS algorithm for a total of 10 times (i.e., repeat step 1 and 2 again for 9 more times) to avoid convergence on a local optimum. Choose the tab (run) that gives the highest value in terms of "R Square" and "Change in Objective Criterion". That is, in each tab (run), go to the "Quality Criteria" heading to click the "R Square" and "Change in Objective Criterion" hyperlink respectively to compare their values.

4. For example, in this PLS-POS calculation, the 7th run (tab) is the best solution because it gives the highest values of these model parameters (0.859 for R^2 and 1.630 for Objective Criterion) among all runs (See Figure 55 and 56).

Figure 55: Checking the R^2

	Original Sample R- Average Weighted	POS Segment 1	POS Segment 2	POS Segment 3	POS Segment 4
CXSAT	0.286	0.771	0.670	0.916	0.777	0.702
LOYAL	0.590	0.859	0.864	0.880	0.920	0.755

Figure 56: Checking the Objective Criterion

5. Next, we go to "Final Results" heading and click the "Segment Sizes" hyperlink to check the segment size. Look at the 2nd tab for their relative segment sizes (see Figure 57):

Figure 57: Segment Sizes (Relative)

Segment Sizes

	Segment Sizes (Total)		Segment Sizes (Relative)		
	Group 1	Group 2	Group 3	Group 4
Percentage:	24.742	27.835	23.711	23.711

6. We build a table to summarize the findings in PLS-POS (see Figure 58):

Figure 58: PLS-POS Model summary (R^2)

	R^2 Values					PLS-POS Weighted Average R^2 Values
	Full Data Set (Original Sample)	PLS-POS Segment 1	PLS-POS Segment 2	PLS-POS Segment 3	PLS-POS Segment 4	
CXSAT	0.286	0.670	0.916	0.777	0.702	0.771
LOYAL	0.590	0.864	0.890	0.920	0.755	0.859

7. From Figure 58, since the "PLS-POS Weighted Average R^2 Values" are significantly larger than the "Full Dataset's R^2 Values", we

argue that a "4-segment" solution is preferred as it has higher predictive power than having a solution without segmentation.

8. Becker et al., (2013) have stated that each segment should be **differentiable**. Using PLS-POS, we can test the significance of differences in path coefficients between segments. If a segment is not really different from one another, the researcher should consider combining it with another segment. To check the Path Coefficient, go to the "Final Results" heading and select "Path Coefficients". Then, select the corresponding tab (e.g., Original Path Coefficient, POS Segment 1, POS Segment 2, POS Segment 3 and POS Segment 4) to view their respective path coefficients. Summarize the data in a table format (see Figure 59).

Figure 59: PLS-POS Model Summary (Path coefficients)

	Full Data Set (Original Path Coefficient)	POS Segment 1	POS Segment 2	POS Segment 3	POS Segment 4
CXSAT → LOYAL	0.446	0.455	-0.882	1.088	1.270
CXSATq → LOYAL	-0.020	-0.082	-0.412	0.245	0.073
EXPECT → CXSAT	0.128	1.143	0.258	-0.042	-0.916
EXPECT → LOYAL	0.211	0.322	0.241	-0.136	1.194
QUAL → CXSAT	0.442	-0.554	0.747	0.909	0.771
QUAL → LOYAL	0.246	0.229	1.209	0.161	-0.404

9. It can be seen that in Segment 1, CXSAT has a positive impact on LOYAL (0.455) but CXSAT has a negative impact on LOYAL (-0.882) in Segment 2. Meanwhile, EXPECT has a positive impact on LOYAL in Segment 1, 2 and 4 but it has a negative impact on LOYAL (-0.136) in segment 3. It has also been observed that QUAL has a positive impact on LOYAL in segment 1, 2, and 3 but it has a negative impact on LOYAL (-0.404) in Segment 4.

10. Once the PLS-POS results are generated, we can perform the ex-post analysis to interpret and characterize the segments obtained, using explanatory variables in the model/theory. In other words, we want to identify explanatory variables that match well with the PLS-POS partition.

(iii) Ex-post Analysis

1. Open the "cafe100.csv" data file in Excel. Now, delete all observations with missing values. In this case, we have 3 observations with missing values, so our resulting dataset has 97 observations. Save this file as "cafe97.csv" and keep opening it in Excel.

2. In SmartPLS' PLS-POS result page, go to the "Final Results" heading and click the "Segment Assignment" hyperlink.

3. Press the "Excel Format" button[59] on the right-hand side to copy the Final Partition information to the clipboard (see Figure 60).

Figure 60: Segment Assignment

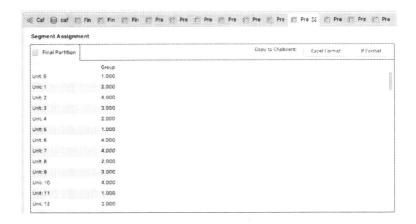

4. Paste this data from clipboard to the next available column on the right-hand side of your data in the "cafe97.csv" file. Rename that column as "PLS-POS Groups" (see Figure 61):

---

[59] This "Export to Excel" function is only available in the paid version of SmartPLS 3. If you are using a student version, just copy and paste the values manually onto your spreadsheet.

Figure 61: Adding Segment Assignment Information to the Data File.

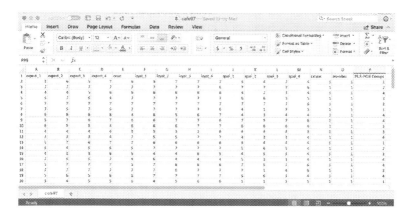

5. Our goal is to compare the PLS-POS segments or partitions with those identified by other observable variables in the original dataset. Using statistical software like SPSS, import the data from this "cafe97.csv" file, and run a "Crosstab" analysis[60] to show how these categories are related to each other.

6. In our dataset, we have 2 observable variables; *cxtype* determines if the café patron is a student or not, whereas *member* determines if the café patron is a loyalty program member or not. We can compare them one by one.

7. To begin with, we compare our PLS-POS Groups with *cxtype* in SPSS' cross tab. (see Figure 62 & 63)

---

[60] In SPSS, select Analyze → Descriptive Statistics → Crosstabs…

Figure 62: Running Crosstab in SPSS (cxtype vs. PLSPOS_Groups)

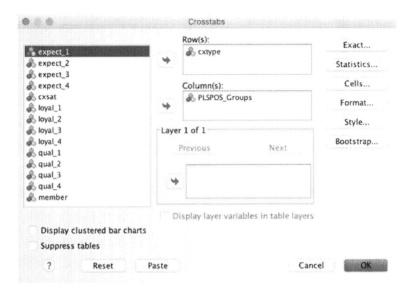

Figure 63: Crosstab Result (Cxtype vs. PLSPOS_Groups)

cxtype * PLSPOS_Groups Crosstabulation

			PLSPOS_Groups				
			1	2	3	4	Total
cxtype	1	Count	10	11	8	14	43
		% within cxtype	23.3%	25.6%	18.6%	32.6%	100.0%
		% within PLSPOS_Groups	41.7%	40.7%	34.8%	60.9%	44.3%
	2	Count	14	16	15	9	54
		% within cxtype	25.9%	29.6%	27.8%	16.7%	100.0%
		% within PLSPOS_Groups	58.3%	59.3%	65.2%	39.1%	55.7%
Total		Count	24	27	23	23	97
		% within cxtype	24.7%	27.8%	23.7%	23.7%	100.0%
		% within PLSPOS_Groups	100.0%	100.0%	100.0%	100.0%	100.0%

8. Then, we compare our PLS-POS Groups with *member* in SPSS' cross tab (see Figure 64 & 65).

Figure 64: Running Crosstab in SPSS (member vs. PLSPOS_Groups)

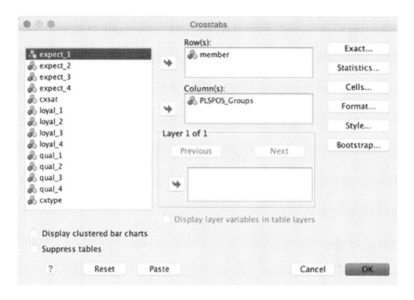

Figure 65: Crosstab Result (member vs. PLSPOS_Groups)

member * PLSPOS_Groups Crosstabulation

			PLSPOS_Groups				
			1	2	3	4	Total
member	1	Count	14	15	9	11	49
		% within member	28.6%	30.6%	18.4%	22.4%	100.0%
		% within PLSPOS_Groups	58.3%	55.6%	39.1%	47.8%	50.5%
	2	Count	10	12	14	12	48
		% within member	20.8%	25.0%	29.2%	25.0%	100.0%
		% within PLSPOS_Groups	41.7%	44.4%	60.9%	52.2%	49.5%
Total		Count	24	27	23	23	97
		% within member	24.7%	27.8%	23.7%	23.7%	100.0%
		% within PLSPOS_Groups	100.0%	100.0%	100.0%	100.0%	100.0%

9. At this point, the researcher has to decide if the "number of segments" make any sense in reality. We want to ensure the retained segments are theoretically **plausible**.[61] An important concept here is to turn unobserved heterogeneity into observed

---

[61] Differentiable segments that are not plausible may be outliers and thus should not be retained.

heterogeneity by making the segment **accessible**. This can be done by finding additional variables beyond the original model/theory to explain the plausible segments that are retained. Specifically, we may want to delete, add, or combine one or more segments for our subsequent analysis.

10. From both Figure 63 and Figure 65, it can be seen that Group #1 and #2 are very similar in terms of their "% within PLSPOS_Groups", so perhaps we can consider combining them into a single segment and call it "Segment 1". The majority of this combined segment (with 51 café patrons) are non-students and member of the loyalty program.

11. For Group #3, most café patrons are non-students (65.2%) and non-member of the loyalty program (60.9%). Meanwhile, most café patrons in Group #4 are students (60.9%) and non-members (52.2%)[62]. We can summarize these findings in the following Figure 66:

Figure 66: Revised Segments

Revised Segments	Number of patrons	Coming from PLS-POS	Revised Segment Descriptions (i.e., New Data Group name)
1	51	Group #1 + Group #2	Non-student + member
2	23	Group #3	Non-student + non-member
3	23	Group #4	Student + non-member

12. Now, go back to SmartPLS to set up new data groups for PLS-SEM estimation. Recall that we now have a new dataset with only 97 observations, so we go to the "Project Explorer" tab and right click the blue-color "cafe100" icon. In the pop-up window, select

---

[62] Usually, we prefer to have at least 60% overlap between the explanatory variable and the POS-PLS partition. However, for the sake of this demonstration, we will accept a slightly lower value of 52.2% to show that Group 4 has more non-members than members.

the "cafe97.csv" data file and press OK. This "cafe97 [97 records]" file should now be highlighted.

13. Click the "Add Data Group" icon at the top. A new window called "Configure Data Group" appears. Type "Non-student + member" in the "Group Name:" box and set "PLS-POS Groups" is lower than 3, as in Figure 67, and then press "OK".

Figure 67: Configure Data Group (Non-student + Member)

14. Following the same process, create the other 2 new segments (see Figure 68 & 69).

Figure 68: Configure Data Group (Non-student + Non-member)

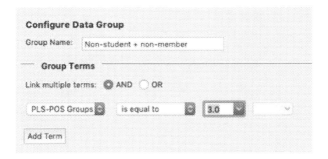

Figure 69: Configure Data Group (Student + Non-member)

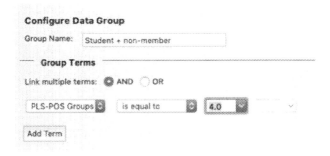

15. The final step is segment-specific model estimation. Assuming we are satisfied with the defined Data Groups, we can proceed to estimate the PLS path model for each data group separately. First, click the colorful model tab, then go to the "Calculate" menu and select "PLS Algorithm". In the "Data Groups" tab, select the corresponding groups and start calculation (see Figure 70).

Figure 70: Running PLS-SEM Algorism Using New Data Groups

Partial Least Squares Algorithm

The PLS path modeling method was developed by Wol
vectors obtained at convergence satisfy fixed point equ

| ⚙ Setup | 👥 Weighting | 👥 Data Groups | |

Run algorithm for the following selected data groups:

☑ Select All
☑ Non-student + member   51 cases
☑ Non-student + non-member   23 cases
☑ Student + non-member   23 cases

16. In the "Data Group:" pull-down menu, select the first group called "Non-student + member". Do not press the "next" button or else you will be viewing the next group's result (see Figure 71).

Figure 71: Viewing the Corresponding Group Result

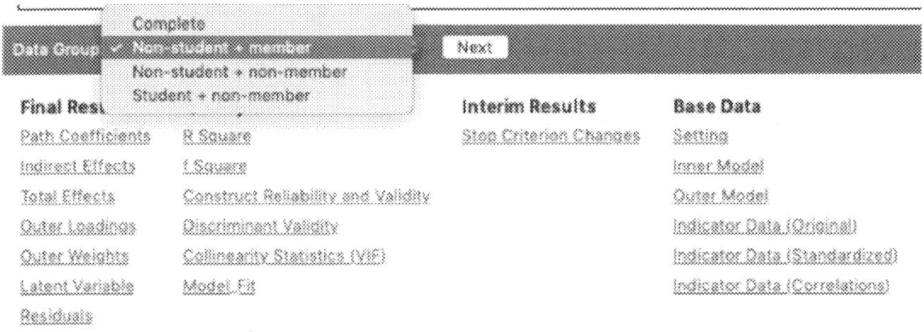

17. We also need to separately run bootstrapping for each segment and then compare path coefficient between them. That means click the colorful model tab, go to the "Calculate" menu and perform a "Bootstrapping" procedure using the default setting parameters. Assuming you have selected all groups in the "Data Group" tab, this bootstrapping procedure will be carried out for all segments simultaneously.

18. The "Original Sample (O)" column shows the path coefficients for the aggregate model under the "Data Group: Complete" setting (see Figure 72).

Figure 72: Path Coefficients (Complete)

Path Coefficients (Complete)

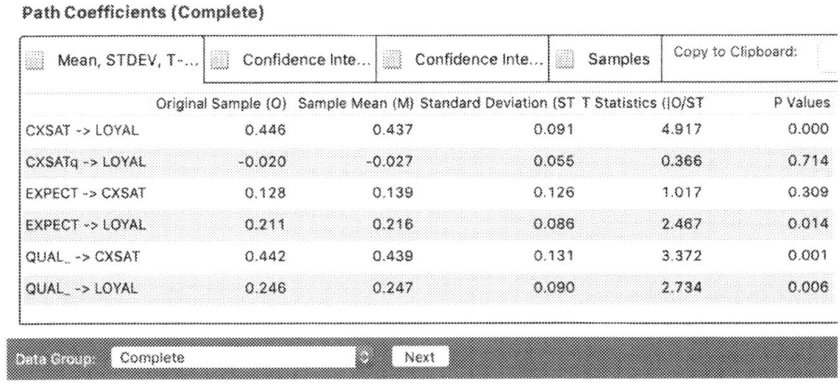

	Original Sample (O)	Sample Mean (M)	Standard Deviation (STDEV)	T Statistics (|O/STDEV|)	P Values
CXSAT -> LOYAL	0.446	0.437	0.091	4.917	0.000
CXSATq -> LOYAL	-0.020	-0.027	0.055	0.366	0.714
EXPECT -> CXSAT	0.128	0.139	0.126	1.017	0.309
EXPECT -> LOYAL	0.211	0.216	0.086	2.467	0.014
QUAL_ -> CXSAT	0.442	0.439	0.131	3.372	0.001
QUAL_ -> LOYAL	0.246	0.247	0.090	2.734	0.006

19. Select other segments in the pull-down menu to view their path coefficients.

20. Once that is done, check the R^2 for these 3 newly formed segments. To do this, first click the colorful model tab. Go to the "Calculate" menu and select "PLS Algorithm". In the Data Groups tab, only select the first group "Non-student + member". Press "Start Calculation" (see Figure 73).

Figure 73: Performing PLS Algorithm Using Selected Data Group

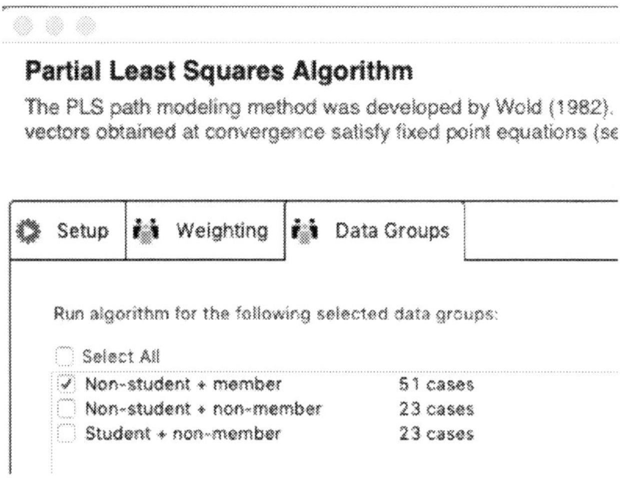

21. Repeat this PLS Algorithm process one-by-one for the remaining 2 segments to get the R^2. We can also calculate the weighted R^2 by considering the group's relative segment size.[63] Since we make use of the reflective measurement model type[64], we should also check the model's (i) Convergent validity (AVE), (ii) Reliability (composite reliability, Cronbach's alpha, rho_A), and (iii)

---

[63] For example, the weighted R^2 for CXSAT is (0.490 * 52.6%) + (0.777 * 23.7%) + (0.702* 23.7%) = 0.608. Similarly, the weighted R^2 for LOYAL is (0.697*52.6%) + (0.920*23.7%) + (0.755*23.7%) = 0.764.

[64] If the formative measurement model type is used as well, researcher should also check (i) Convergent validity, (ii) Collinearity, and (iii) Significance and relevance of the indicators. See Wong (2013).

Discriminant validity ($HTMT_{inference}$). Summarize the data in a table like the one in Figure 74.

Figure 74: Final Segmentation Result

	Complete (Original sample without segmentation)	Segment 1: Non-student + member	Segment 2: Non-student + non-member	Segment 3: Student + non-member
N	97	51	23	23
Relative Segment Size	100.0%	52.6%	23.7%	23.7%
Path Coefficient				
CXSAT → LOYAL	0.446***	0.167	1.088***	1.270***
CXSATq → LOYAL	-0.020	-0.158**	0.245*	0.073
EXPECT → CXSAT	0.128	0.596***	-0.042	-0.916***
EXPECT → LOYAL	0.211**	0.197	-0.136	1.194***
QUAL → CXSAT	0.442***	0.139	0.909***	0.771***
QUAL → LOYAL	0.246***	0.433***	0.161	-0.404
Reflective measures				
Convergent validity	+	+	+	+
Reliability	+	+	+	+
Discriminant validity	+	+	+	+
R^2				
CXSAT	0.286	0.490	0.777	0.702
LOYAL	0.590	0.697	0.920	0.755
Weighted R^2				
CXSAT	0.286	0.608		
LOYAL	0.590	0.764		

*** $p \leq 0.01$
** $p \leq 0.05$
* $p \leq 0.10$

22. From Figure 74, it can be seen that the weighted R^2 (0.608 and 0.764) are larger than the original R^2 for both CXSAT (0.286) and LOYAL (0.590) respectively. This clearly illustrates that grouping the data using the chosen explanatory variables increases the model's in-sample predictive power, as compared to the aggregate, combined level analysis.

Comparing the path coefficients among the 3 segments in Figure 74, it is obvious that these segments are different in terms of their structural model effects. For example, the most important factor that leads to customer loyalty is QUAL (0.433, $p \leq 0.01$) for segment 1. However, it is CXSAT that drives loyalty the most in segment 2 (1.088, $p \leq 0.01$) and segment 3 (1.270, $p \leq 0.01$)

respectively. Meanwhile, in the original homogenous sample, EXPECT has a significant effect on LOYAL (0.211, p≤0.05), but the same can only be said for segment 3 (1.194, p≤0.01) and not in segment 1 or 2. This completes the segment-specific model estimation.

23. Using these results, the café owner can draw some **managerial implications**. For example, about half of the patrons being surveyed hold loyalty card membership and this customer segment cares more about perceived quality (QUAL) than other aspects of the business. Hence, the café owner should prioritize to ensure it has tasty food, friendly servers, accurate billing, and well-crafted drinks. On the other hand, if the café owner believes that students play a strategic role in the future growth of her café, she need to focus on improving customer expectation (EXPECT) because it is the second most important factor in driving loyalty after customer satisfaction (CXSAT). That is, the owner should make sure her café has best menu selection, great atmospheric elements, good looking servers and affordable daily specials.

24. In the ideal scenario, marketing researcher should consider validating their segmentation results with other data that are not used in the estimation process, and/or repeating the segmentation analysis on another population. By using external data or collecting addition data in a follow-up study, researcher can test the proposed explanatory variables to make the research results more generalizable with the ultimate goal of refining the theory.

CHAPTER 9

Estimating Complex Models Using Higher Order Construct Modeling (HCM)

Case Study: Customer Survey in a Photocopier Manufacturer (B2B)

Since PLS-SEM is a relatively new approach to modeling, researchers who are not familiar with it may find the analytical and reporting aspects challenging, especially in the areas of higher-order constructs modeling, mediation analysis, and categorical moderation analysis. Chapter 9, 10 and 11 are written to help researchers master these skill sets by demonstrating the mentioned analyses through a fictitious B2B research example in the photocopier industry. PLS-SEM model estimation was performed in SmartPLS 2.0M3 software (Ringle, C. M., Wende, S., & Will, A., 2005), whereas data preparation will be performed in Microsoft Excel and IBM SPSS.

Conceptual Framework and Research Hypotheses

In this research example, a researcher named Susan is the marketing vice president of a photocopier manufacturer. The company's business customers include organizations in both non-profit and for-profit sectors. Susan is interested in learning more about the driving forces behind customer loyalty, particularly factors such as brand reputation, pricing, and customer satisfaction. Susan has previously attended an EMBA course on brand reputation, and she recalled the 5 underlying indicators that contribute to a company's brand reputation; they are corporate social responsibility, financial performance, governance, leadership, and product/service quality. Susan is interested in carrying out a structural equation modeling exercise because her goal is to understand the relationships among these factors. Based on this information, Susan developed the conceptual framework for her research project (see Figure 75).

Figure 75: Conceptual Framework

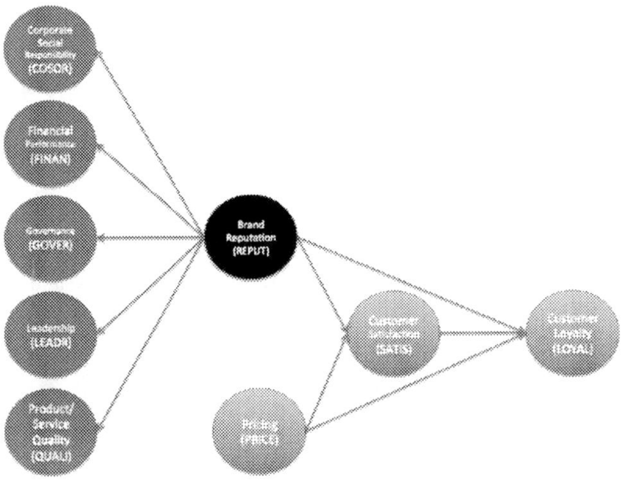

Questionnaire Design and Data Collection

A questionnaire is designed around each latent construct of interest. Susan's business customers are asked to provide feedback in major areas that reflect the latent constructs in the model. Using a measurement scale from 0 to 10 (totally disagree to fully agree), business customers are asked to evaluate each statement (i.e., the indicator variable) such as "This company offers good after-sales service." in the questionnaire. Since brand reputation is a higher-order construct, it is evaluated by asking questions surrounding the 5 underlying factors. The statements to be evaluated are:

Quality (QUALI)
[This company] offers reliable, high-quality photocopier.
[This company] offers good after-sales service.

Corporate Social Responsibility (COSOR)
[This company] sponsors community events and programs.
[This company] maintains production processes that minimize the impact to the environment.

Financial Performance (FINAN)
[This company] is a high-performance company, it delivers strong financial results.
[This company] delivers above-market-average share price performance.
[This company] has a comfortable cash position.

Governance (GOVER)
[This company] behaves ethically and is open and transparent in its business dealings.
[This company] has good internal control.
[This company] maintains full compliance in its financial disclosures and reports.

Leadership (LEADR)
[This company] has a strong, visible leader.
[This company] is managed effectively.
The senior management is well known for its good relationship with its employees.

Pricing (PRICE)
The price is reasonable.
The total cost of ownership reasonable.

Customer Loyalty (LOYAL)
I would recommend [this company] to other business partners.
If I had to select again, I would choose [this company] as my photocopier supplier.
I will remain a customer of [this company] in the future.

Customer Satisfaction (SATIS)
Overall, I am satisfied with the product and service provided by [this company].

A total of 200 questionnaires are received from Susan's business customers; 106 of them are non-profit organizations (including government agencies) whereas the rest are for-profit companies. Luckily, the collected questionnaires contain no missing data.

Hypotheses Development

Once the conceptual framework is finalized, the next step is hypotheses development. The first hypothesis is developed to explore the relationship between brand reputation and loyalty:

H_1: Brand reputation (REPUT) significantly influences customer loyalty (LOYAL)
The second hypothesis is developed to examine the relationship between brand reputation and customer satisfaction:
H_2: Brand reputation (REPUT) significantly influences customer satisfaction (SATIS)
The third and fourth hypotheses are created to explore the relationship between pricing and customer loyalty, and those between pricing and customer satisfaction, respectively:
H_3: Pricing (PRICE) significantly influences customer loyalty (LOYAL)
H_4: Pricing (PRICE) significantly influences customer satisfaction (SATIS)
The fifth hypothesis is created to test the linkage between customer satisfaction and customer loyalty:
H_5: Customer satisfaction (SATIS) significantly influences customer loyalty (LOYAL)
Customer satisfaction is an endogenous variable in the model. Other latent constructs such as brand reputation and pricing are hypothesized to influence customer satisfaction, which in turn affects customer loyalty. The potential mediating effect of customer satisfaction on other constructs are of interest in Susan's research and hence the sixth and seventh hypothesis are developed as the followings:

H_6: Customer satisfaction (SATIS) significantly mediates the relationship between brand reputation (REPUT) and customer loyalty (LOYAL)

H_7: Customer satisfaction (SATIS) significantly mediates the relationship between pricing (PRICE) and customer loyalty (LOYAL)

Susan is also interested in understanding if her findings in this PLS-SEM research can be applied to both non-profit and for-profit organizations. To confirm such insights, the last hypothesis of this research is developed to test the categorical moderating effect of business type (i.e., non-profit vs. for-profit) in the model:

H_8: There is significant categorical moderating effect of business type on the relationship among model constructs.

We will explore mediation analysis later in Chapter 10, followed by categorical moderation analysis in Chapter 11.

PLS-SEM Design Considerations

Sample size

In Susan's research project, there are 200 participants (N=106 non-profit organizations; N=94 for-profit organizations). This sample size satisfies both the "10 times rule"[65] (Thompson, Barclay, & Higgins, 1995) and the guidelines[66] as suggested by Hair, Hult, Ringle, & Sarstedt (2013).

Multiple-item vs. Single-item Indicators

This research originally includes a total of 19 indicator variables. Since the sample size is larger than 50, the indicating variables are designed to make use of multiple-item instead of single-item to measure the latent construct (Diamantopoulos, Sarstedt, Fuchs, Kaiser, & Wilczynski, 2012). Other than customer satisfaction (SATIS) which is a single-item construct, all others are each measured by 2 to 3 indicators (i.e., questionnaire questions).

---

[65] The "10 times rule" suggest that sample size should at least equal to "10 times the maximum number of structural paths pointing at a latent variable anywhere in the PLS path model". That is, 10 x 3 structural paths = 30 business customers.

[66] One would need at least 59 observations to achieve a statistical power of 80% for detecting R-square values of at least 0.25.

Formative vs. Reflective Hierarchical Components Model

According to Lohmöller (1989), PLS-SEM can be designed as a hierarchical components model (HCM)[67] that includes the observable lower-order components (LOCs) and unobservable higher-order components (HOCs) to reduce model complexity and make it more theoretical parsimony.

In Susan's photocopier research, it is designed as a reflective-reflective hierarchical component model (rr-HCM)[68]. Specifically, the HOC brand reputation holds a reflective relationship with its LOCs (quality, corporate social responsibility, financial performance, governance, and leadership) that are measured by reflective indicators that hang well together. This model design is in line with prior research regarding reputation for company (Hair et al., 2013, p235).

Data Preparation for SmartPLS

Prior to running PLS model estimation in SmartPLS, Susan has to manually type the questionnaire data into Microsoft Excel with the names of those indicators (e.g., loyal_1, loyal_2, loyal_3) being placed in the first row of an Excel spreadsheet. Each row represents an individual questionnaire response, with number from 0 to 10. Since there are 200 responses, there should be 201 rows in the spreadsheet (see Figure 76). The file has to be saved in the specific "CSV (Comma Delimited)" format in Excel[69] because SmartPLS cannot import .xls or .xlsx files directly.

---

[67] The use of hierarchical component model can also reduce bias due to collinearity issues and eliminate potential discriminant validity problems. See Hair et al. (2013, p229).

[68] The hierarchical components model is formative or reflective depends on whether the researcher is trying to (i) mediate the relationships between the lower-order constructs (LOCs) and their target constructs in the path modeling (→ formative), or (ii) use a single latent entity to represent all the LOCs in order to simplify the model (→ reflective).

[69] To do this, go to the "File" menu in Excel, and choose "CSV (Comma Delimited)" as the file format type to save it onto your computer. See Wong (2013) for a step-by-step instruction.

Figure 76: Data Entry in Microsoft Excel

	A	B	C	D	E	F	G	H	I	J	K
1	loyal_1	loyal_2	loyal_3	satis_1	price_1	price_2	quali_1	quali_2	brand_1	brand_2	brand_3
2	7	7	3	6	1	7	7	7	4	1	6
3	4	1	1	3	2	4	3	7	3	1	7
4	7	7	3	4	5	5	3	7	5	2	6
5	5	4	3	6	4	6	6	4	6	4	7
6	5	5	5	7	7	6	5	7	6	3	6
7	7	4	6	7	3	6	4	7	6	1	4
8	5	6	4	5	2	4	4	6	4	2	4
9	6	5	4	6	4	6	3	6	3	4	7
10	5	5	2	5	3	6	6	5	5	3	4
11	6	7	1	5	7	6	5	7	7	6	5
12	1	1	4	5	6	1	1	6	3	1	4
13	4	1	1	4	4	4	4	4	4	4	4
14	7	3	1	5	1	5	3	7	7	1	6
15	2	1	7	3	7	2	6	3	4	3	6
16	4	4	7	7	7	7	6	6	6	1	7
17	4	6	5	6	6	5	4	3	5	4	6
18	5	5	1	5	7	4	4	7	7	1	7
19	6	4	4	5	5	5	5	6	5	3	4
20	5	4	3	4	5	5	3	4	3	3	2
21	2	2	3	6	7	7	2	7	7	1	6
22	4	6	4	6	7	7	7	7	7	1	7
23	4	5	3	2	4	6	6	6	4	3	5

Data Analysis and Results

PLS Path Model Estimation

Susan designs the PLS model in SmartPLS based on the conceptual framework mentioned earlier. The HOC, brand reputation, is drawn using the "repeated indicators approach"[70]. Once the model is drawn, the indicator data can be imported into the SmartPLS software[71] (see Figure 77).

---

[70] Indicators from lower-order components (e.g., COSOR, FINAN, GOVER, LEADR and QUALI) are deployed again for the corresponding higher-order component (e.g., REPUT).

[71] This can be done by right clicking on the "photocopier.splsm" file in the "Projects" window, and then select "Import Indicator Data".

Figure 77: Importing Indicator Data

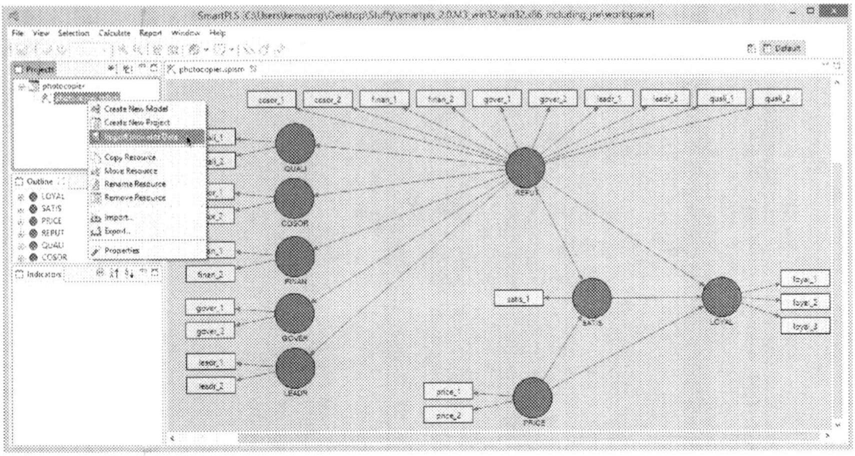

The PLS-SEM algorithm is run[72] and successfully converged[73] within the guideline suggested by Hair et al., (2013). Before Susan can properly assess the path coefficients in the structural model, she must first examine the indicator reliability, internal consistency reliability, discriminant validity, and convergent validity of the reflective measurement model to ensure they are satisfactory (Wong, 2013).

Indicator Reliability

Since reliability is a condition for validity, indicator reliability is first checked to ensure the associated indicators have much in common that is captured by the latent construct. After examining the outer loadings for all latent variables[74], the 2 indicators that form COSOR are removed because their outer loadings are smaller than the 0.4 threshold level (Hair

---

[72] By going to the "Calculate → PLS Algorithm".

[73] The PLS-SEM algorithm should converge in iteration lower than the maximum number of iterations (e.g. 300) as set in the algorithm parameter settings; in this PLS Path model estimation, the algorithm successfully converged after Iteration 8 (see Report → Default Report → PLS → Calculation Results → Stop Criterion Changes).

[74] For brand reputation, the outer loadings for higher-order construct (REPUT) instead of lower-order construct (i.e., QUALI, COSOR, GOVER...etc.) are examined (see Hair et al, 2013, p235).

et al, 2013). Meanwhile, 3 indicators (Finan_2, Gover_2, and Leadr_1) are found to have loadings between 0.4 to 0.7. A loading relevance test[75] is therefore performed for these 3 indicators to see if they should be retained in the model. As the elimination of these 3 indicators would result in an increase of Average Variance Extracted (AVE) and composite reliability of their respective latent construct, they are removed from the PLS model. The remaining indicators are retained because their outer loadings are all 0.7 or higher[76]. The PLS algorithm is re-run. The resulting path model estimation is presented in Figure 78 and the outer loadings of various constructs are shown in Figure 79:

Figure 78: PLS Path Model Estimation

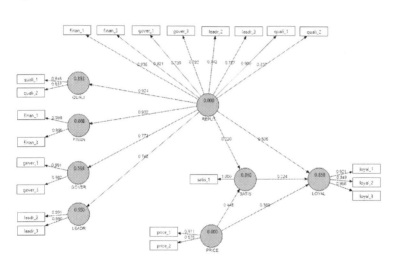

---

[75] In a loading relevance test, problematic indicators should be deleted only if their removal from the PLS model leads to an increase of AVE and composite reliability of their constructs over the 0.5 thresholds. These figures can be obtained from the software by viewing "Report → Default report → PLS→ Quality Criteria → Overview".

[76] An indicator's outer loading should be 0.708 or above since that number squared (0.708^2) equals 0.50, meaning the latent variable should be able to explain at least 50% of each indicator's variance.

Figure 79: Outer Loadings

Constructs (Latent Variables)	Outer loadings
Brand Reputation (REPUT)	
Quality (QUALI)	
Quali_1 [This company] offers reliable, high-quality photocopier	0.900
Quali_2 [This company] offers good after-sales service	0.837
Financial Performance (FINAN)	
Finan_1 [This company] is a high-performance company, it delivers strong financial results	0.935
Finan_3 [This company] has a comfortable cash position	0.921
Governance (GOVER)	
Gover_1 [This company] behaves ethically and is open and transparent in its business dealings	0.739
Gover_3 [This company] maintains full compliance in its financial disclosures and reports	0.792
Leadership (LEADR)	
Leadr_2 [This company] is managed effectively	0.742
Leadr_3 The senior management is well known for its good relationship with its employees	0.727
Pricing (PRICE)	
Price_1 The price is reasonable	0.911
Price_2 The total cost of ownership reasonable	0.676
Customer Loyalty (LOYAL)	
Loyal_1 I would recommend [this company] to other business partners	0.921
Loyal_2 If I had to select again, I would choose [this company] as my photocopier supplier	0.849
Loyal_3 I will remain a customer of [this company] in the future	0.966
Customer Satisfaction (SATIS)	
Satis_1 Overall, I am satisfied with the product and service provided by [this company]	1

Internal Consistency Reliability

In this PLS-SEM example, composite reliability rather than Cronbach's alpha[77] is used to evaluate the measurement model's internal consistency reliability.[78] This is because it takes into consideration of the different outer loadings of the indicators (Werts, Linn, & Joreskog, 1974). In Susan's

---

[77] The internal consistency reliability is traditionally checked using Cronbach's alpha. However, it is not suitable for PLS-SEM because it is sensitive to the number of items in the scale, and this measure is also found to generate severe underestimation when applied to PLS path models (see Werts, Linn, & Joreskog, 1974).

[78] As discussed in the book earlier, rho_A coefficient can also be used to check reliability

research, the composite reliability[79] for the constructs REPUT, PRICE and LOYAL are shown to be 0.9454, 0.7791, and 0.9378 respectively, indicating high levels of internal consistency reliability[80] (Nunnally & Bernstein, 1994). Please note that the value of SATIS is 1.00 but it does not imply perfection in composite reliability because it is a single-item variable.

Convergent Validity

Convergent validity refers to the model's ability to explain the indicator's variance. The AVE can provide evidence[81] for convergent validity (Fornell and Larcker, 1981). The AVE for the latent construct LOYAL, PRICE, and REPUT are 0.8343, 0.6432, and 0.6859 respectively, well above the required minimum level of 0.50 (Bagozzi and Yi, 1988). Therefore, the measures of the three reflective constructs can be said to have high levels of convergent validity.

Discriminant Validity

As discussed previously in the book, the Fornell-Larcker criterion (1981) is a traditional and common approach to assess discriminant validity[82] although it gives conservative results as compared to the modern approach of using HTMT (see Chapter 12 if HTMT is chosen to check discriminant validity).

---

[79] If there is a HOC, only consider the composite reliability of the HOC (e.g., REPUT) and not its LOC (e.g., QUALI, FINAN, GOVER and LEADR).

[80] Prior research suggests that a threshold level of 0.60 or higher is required to demonstrate a satisfactory composite reliability in exploratory research (Bagozzi and Yi, 1988) but not exceeding the 0.95 level (Hair et al., 2013).

[81] Bagozzi and Yi (1988) suggest an AVE threshold level of 0.5 as evidence of convergent validity. Two of our constructs exceeded this level and the rest are not too far away from this level. Since all of these constructs met discriminant validity and other reliability tests, they are kept in the model to maintain content validity.

[82] Another method is cross-loading examination, in which the indicator's loading to its latent construct should be higher than that of other constructs. See "Reports → Default Report → PLS → Quality Criteria → Cross Loadings".

If the Fornell-Larcker criterion is used, the AVE should be checked. That is, in order to establish the discriminant validity[83], the square root of average variance extracted (AVE) of each latent variable should be larger than the latent variable correlations (LVC). Figure 80 clearly shows that discriminant validity is met for this research because the square root of AVE for REPUT, PRICE, SATIS and LOYAL are much larger than the corresponding LVC[84].

Figure 80: Fornell-Larcker Criterion

Latent Variable Correlations (LVC)					Discriminant Validity met? (Square root of AVE>LVC?)
	LOYAL	PRICE	REPUT	SATIS	
LOYAL	*0.9134*				Yes
PRICE	0.7883	*0.8020*			Yes
REPUT	0.8245	0.5769	*0.8282*		Yes
SATIS	0.6760	0.5722	0.4772	Single-item	Yes

Note: The square root of AVE values is shown on the diagonal and printed in italics; non-diagonal elements are the latent variable correlations (LVC).

Collinearity Assessment

In addition to checking the measurement model, the structural model has to be properly evaluated before drawing any conclusion. Collinearity is a potential issue in the structural model and that variance inflation factor (VIF) value of 5 or above typically indicates such problem (Hair et al., 2011). Since SmartPLS does not generate the VIF value, another piece of statistical software such as IBM SPSS has to be utilized. This procedure

---

[83] If there is a HOC, only consider the discriminant validity of the HOC (e.g., REPUT) and not its LOC (e.g., QUALI, FINAN, GOVER and LEADR).
[84] To find LVC values, go to "Reports → Default report → PLS → Quality criteria → Latent variable correlation".

involves a few easy steps. First, generate the latent variables scores[85] in SmartPLS (see Figure 81).

Figure 81: Latent Variables Scores

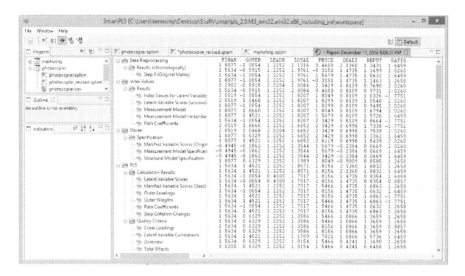

Then, copy the data into Microsoft Excel, save it in "CSV (Comma Delimited)" format and then open it in IBM SPSS (see Figure 82).

---

[85] Go to "Report → PLS → calculation results → Latent Variable Scores"

Figure 82: Data in SPSS

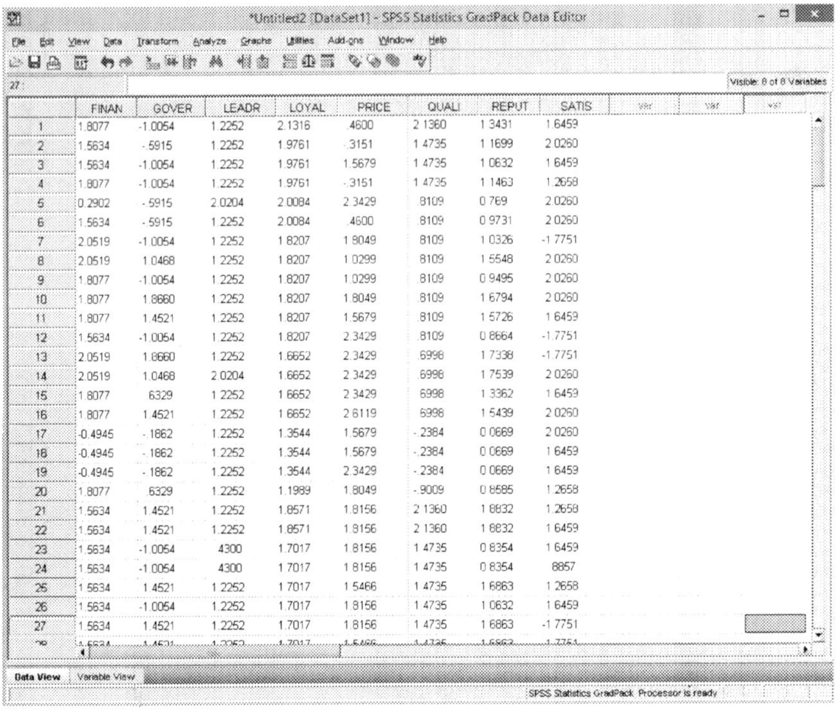

*Untitled2 [DataSet1] - SPSS Statistics GradPack Data Editor

	FINAN	GOVER	LEADR	LOYAL	PRICE	QUALI	REPUT	SATIS
1	1.8077	-1.0054	1.2252	2.1316	.4600	2.1360	1.3431	1.6459
2	1.5634	-.5915	1.2252	1.9761	-.3151	1.4735	1.1699	2.0260
3	1.5634	-1.0054	1.2252	1.9761	1.5679	1.4735	1.0632	1.6459
4	1.8077	-1.0054	1.2252	1.9761	-.3151	1.4735	1.1463	1.2658
5	0.2902	-.5915	2.0204	2.0084	2.3429	.8109	0.769	2.0260
6	1.5634	-.5915	1.2252	2.0084	.4600	.8109	0.9731	2.0260
7	2.0519	-1.0054	1.2252	1.8207	1.8049	8109	1.0326	-1.7751
8	2.0519	1.0468	1.2252	1.8207	1.0299	8109	1.5548	2.0260
9	1.8077	-1.0054	1.2252	1.8207	1.0299	.8109	0.9495	2.0260
10	1.8077	1.8660	1.2252	1.8207	1.8049	.8109	1.6794	2.0260
11	1.8077	1.4521	1.2252	1.8207	1.5679	.8109	1.5726	1.6459
12	1.5634	-1.0054	1.2252	1.8207	2.3429	.8109	0.8664	-1.7751
13	2.0519	1.8660	1.2252	1.6652	2.3429	.6998	1.7338	-1.7751
14	2.0519	1.0468	2.0204	1.6652	2.3429	.6998	1.7539	2.0260
15	1.8077	6329	1.2252	1.6652	2.3429	6998	1.3362	1.6459
16	1.8077	1.4521	1.2252	1.6652	2.6119	6998	1.5439	2.0260
17	-0.4945	-.1862	1.2252	1.3544	1.5679	-.2384	0.0669	2.0260
18	-0.4945	-.1862	1.2252	1.3544	1.5679	-.2384	0.0669	1.6459
19	-0.4945	-.1862	1.2252	1.3544	2.3429	-.2384	0.0669	1.6459
20	1.8077	.6329	1.2252	1.1989	1.8049	-.9009	0.8585	1.2658
21	1.5634	1.4521	1.2252	1.8571	1.8156	2.1360	1.8832	1.2658
22	1.5634	1.4521	1.2252	1.8571	1.8156	2.1360	1.8832	1.6459
23	1.5634	-1.0054	4300	1.7017	1.8156	1.4735	0.8354	1.6459
24	1.5634	-1.0054	4300	1.7017	1.8156	1.4735	0.8354	8857
25	1.5634	1.4521	1.2252	1.7017	1.5466	1.4735	1.6863	1.2658
26	1.5634	-1.0054	1.2252	1.7017	1.8156	1.4735	1.0632	1.6459
27	1.5634	1.4521	1.2252	1.7017	1.8156	1.4735	1.6863	-1.7751

In Susan's PLS model, both LOYAL and SATIS act as dependent variables because they have arrows (paths) pointing toward them. So, we need to run two different sets of linear regression to obtain their corresponding VIF values.

For the first run of linear regression[86], LOYAL is the dependent variable whereas REPUT, PRICE, and SATIS serve as "Independent" variables (see Figure 83).

[86] In SPSS, go to "Analyse → Regression → Linear"

Figure 83: Linear Regression

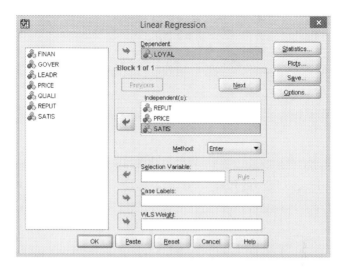

In the Linear Regression window, click the "Statistics…" button and then put a check mark next to "Collinearity diagnostics" (see Figure 84) to obtain the VIF value (see Figure 85).

Figure 84: Linear Regression: Statistics

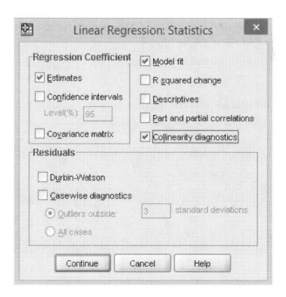

Figure 85: Coefficients Table (First Set)

Coefficients[a]

Model		Unstandardized Coefficients		Standardized Coefficients	t	Sig.	Collinearity Statistics	
		B	Std. Error	Beta			Tolerance	VIF
1	(Constant)	-3.319E-6	.027		.000	1.000		
	REPUT	.505	.034	.505	14.972	.000	.635	1.575
	PRICE	.369	.036	.369	10.210	.000	.553	1.808
	SATIS	.224	.034	.224	6.669	.000	.640	1.562

a. Dependent Variable: LOYAL

For the second set of linear regression, configure SATIS as dependent variable and REPUT and PRICE as independent variables. The VIF values are shown in Figure 86.

Figure 86: Coefficients Table (Second Set)

Coefficients[a]

Model		Unstandardized Coefficients		Standardized Coefficients	t	Sig.	Collinearity Statistics	
		B	Std. Error	Beta			Tolerance	VIF
1	(Constant)	-1.254E-5	.057		.000	1.000		
	REPUT	.220	.070	.220	3.158	.002	.667	1.499
	PRICE	.445	.070	.445	6.378	.000	.667	1.499

a. Dependent Variable: SATIS

The collinearity assessment results are summarized in Figure 87. It can be seen that all VIF values are lower than 5, suggesting that there is no indicative of collinearity between each set of predictor variables.

Figure 87: Collinearity Assessment

First Set			Second Set		
Constructs	VIF	Collinearity Problem? (VIF>5?)	Constructs	VIF	Collinearity Problem? (VIF>5?)
REPUT	1.575	No	REPUT	1.499	No
PRICE	1.808	No	PRICE	1.499	No
SATIS	1.562	No			

Dependent variable: LOYAL   *Dependent variable: SATIS*

Coefficient of Determination (R^2)

A major part of structural model evaluation is the assessment of coefficient of determination (R^2). In Susan's research, LOYAL is the main construct of interest. From the PLS Path model estimation diagram (see Figure 78), the overall R^2 is found to be a strong[87] one, suggesting that the three constructs REPUT, PRICE, and SATIS can jointly explain 85.8% of the variance of the endogenous construct LOYAL[88]. The same model estimation also reveals the R^2 for other latent construct; REPUT and PRICE are found to jointly explain 36.0% of SATIS's variances in this PLS-SEM model.

Path Coefficient

In SmartPLS, the relationships between constructs can be determined by examining their path coefficients and related t statistics via the bootstrapping procedure[89]. From Figure 88, it can be seen that all of the structural model relationships are significant[90], confirming our various hypotheses about the construct relationships. The PLS structural model results enable us to conclude that REPUT has the strongest effect on LOYAL (0.505), followed by PRICE (0.369) and SATIS (0.224).

The PLS model estimation (see Figure 78) also reveals that the high-order construct, REPUT, has strong relationships[91] with its low-order

---

[87] Threshold value of 0.25, 0.5 and 0.7 are often used to describe a weak, moderate, and strong coefficient of determination (Hair at el., 2013)

[88] The R^2 value is 0.858; it is shown inside the blue circle of the LOYAL construct in the PLS diagram (see Figure 74).

[89] Go to "Calculate → bootstrapping" in SmartPLS. Select "200" as cases because there are 200 business customers in this research.

[90] All paths are significant (p<0.01). The t Value is obtained in SmartPLS whereas the corresponding *p* Value is calculated in Microsoft Excel using the TDIST(x,degree of freedom, tails) command, such as TDIST(12.0146,199,2) for the REPUT → LOYAL path.

[91] This means that the lower-order constructs, QUALI, FINAN, GOVER, and LEADR, are highly correlated for the higher-order construct REPUT to explain more than 50% of each LOC's variance.

constructs, QUALI (0.924), FINAN (0.932), GOVER (0.773) and LEADR (0.742).

Figure 88: Significance Testing Results of the Structural Model Path Coefficients

Hypothesis	Path:	Path Coefficients	t Values	Significance Levels	p Values	Hypothesis
H_1	REPUT → LOYAL	0.505	12.0146	***	0.00	Accepted
H_2	REPUT → SATIS	0.220	2.8595	***	0.00	Accepted
H_3	PRICE → LOYAL	0.369	6.7934	***	0.00	Accepted
H_4	PRICE → SATIS	0.445	5.0263	***	0.00	Accepted
H_5	SATIS → LOYAL	0.224	4.0670	***	0.00	Accepted

* $p<0.10$, ** $p<0.05$, *** $p<0.01$

Predictive Relevance (Q^2)

An assessment of Stone-Geisser's predictive relevance (Q^2) is important because it checks if the data points of indicators in the reflective measurement model of the endogenous construct can be predicted accurately. This can be achieved by making use of the blindfolding procedure[92] in SmartPLS (see Figure 89).

---

[92] LOYAL and SATIS are the two endogenous constructs in the model so they are selected for running the Blindfolding Algorithm.

Figure 89: Blindfolding

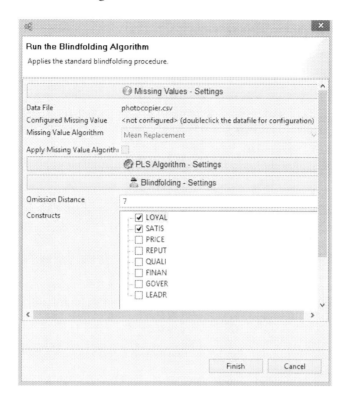

The following table summarizes the results[93]. It is observed that the proposed model has good predictive relevance[94] for all of the endogenous variables (see Figure 90).

Figure 90: Results of Coefficient of Determination (R^2) and Predictive Relevance (Q^2)

Endogenous Latent Variable	R^2 Value	Q^2 Value
LOYAL	0.858	0.709
SATIS	0.360	0.356

---

[93] Q^2 is the "1-SSE/SSO" value as shown in the "Construct Crossvalidated Redundancy" section in blindfolding.

[94] Chin (1998) suggests that a model demonstrates good predictive relevance when its Q^2 value is larger than zero.

The f^2 and q^2 Effect Sizes

The final step in structural model evaluation is to assess the effect of a specific exogenous construct on the endogenous construct if it is deleted from the model. This can be achieved by examining the f^2 and q^2 effect sizes, which can be derived from R^2 and Q^2 respectively[95]. Following Cohan's (1988) guideline[96], it can be said that in general, the exogenous variables have medium to large f^2 and q^2 effect sizes on the endogenous variables (see Figure 91).

Figure 91: Results of f^2 and q^2 Effect Sizes

	LOYAL			SATIS		
	Path Coefficient	f^2 Effect Size	q^2 Effect Size	Path Coefficient	f^2 Effect Size	q^2 Effect Size
REPUT	0.505	0.993	0.444	0.220	0.050	0.053
PRICE	0.369	0.486	0.215	0.445	0.208	0.209
SATIS	0.224	0.225	0.087	n/a	n/a	n/a

Note: Target constructs appear in the first row, whereas the predecessor constructs are in the first column.

---

[95] The f^2 effect size can be calculated manually by taking $(R^2_{included} - R^2_{excluded}) / (1 - R^2_{included})$. Similarly, the q^2 effect size can be calculated by taking $(Q^2_{included} - Q^2_{excluded}) / (1 - Q^2_{included})$.

[96] According to Cohan (1988) f^2 value of 0.02, 0.15, and 0.35 are interpreted as small, medium, and large effect sizes, respectively.

CHAPTER 10

Mediation Analysis

Customer Satisfaction (SATIS) as a Mediator

The relationships among constructs in PLS-SEM can be complex and not always straightforward. To gain a better understanding of the role of SATIS in our model, its potential mediating effect on the linkage between REPUT and LOYAL (see Figure 92), and those between PRICE and LOYAL (see Figure 93) are examined in Susan's research. This is accomplished by following the Preacher and Hayes (2008) procedure[97], which involves the use of bootstrapping in a 2-step procedure: (i) the significance of direct effect is first checked[98] using bootstrapping without the presence of the mediator SATIS in the model[99], and (ii) the significance

---

[97] The Preacher and Hayes (2008) procedure is used instead of the traditional Sobel (1982) test because it does not have strict distributional assumptions (Hair et al, 2013).

[98] If the significance of direct effect cannot be established, there is no mediating effect.

[99] Procedure-wise, go to the "Projects" window, right click on your splsm file, select "Copy resource" to create a revised PLS model in the new window where you can eliminate the SATIS construct. Then, perform a Bootstrapping with 200 cases. The result can be seen at "Report → Default Report → Bootstrapping → Bootstrapping → Path Coefficients (Mean, STDEV, *T*-Values)".

of indirect effect[100] and associated *T*-Values[101] are then checked using the path coefficients when the mediator SATIS is included in the model[102]. This 2-step procedure is performed twice; first for testing the hypothesis six (H_6) and then subsequently for hypothesis seven (H_7). (see Figure 94 and 95)

Figure 92: Mediation Analysis (First Set: H_6)

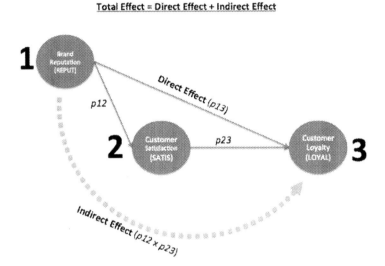

_____

[100] SmartPLS does not calculate the indirect effect values automatically. As such, once the Bootstrapping procedure (with mediator) is completed, copy all 5000 path coefficients (see Default report → Bootstrapping → Bootstrapping → Path Coefficients) to an Excel spreadsheet. Create a column in the spreadsheet as "indirect effect" which is the multiplication result of the 2 paths (*p12* x *p23*). Finally, calculate the Standard Deviation of these 5000 path coefficients by using the Excel command "=STDEV(D4:D5003)" assuming it starts at cell D4. See Figure 12 and 13.

[101] The *T*-Value of indirect effect is calculated by dividing the indirect effect (i.e. *p12* x *p23*) as observed in the PLS model estimation graph by the bootstrapping standard deviation. For example, for REPUT→LOYAL, t = 0.0493/0.0243 = 2.029.

[102] If the significance of indirect effect cannot be established, there is no mediating effect. Having a significant indirect effect is the basis to determine the mediator's magnitude.

Figure 93: Mediation Analysis (Second Set: H₇)

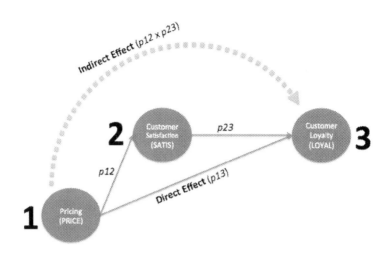

Total Effect = Direct Effect + Indirect Effect

Figure 94: Path Coefficients from Bootstrapping

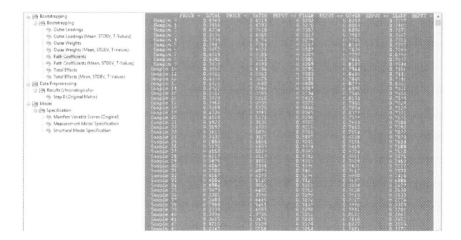

Figure 95: Calculating STDEV in Excel

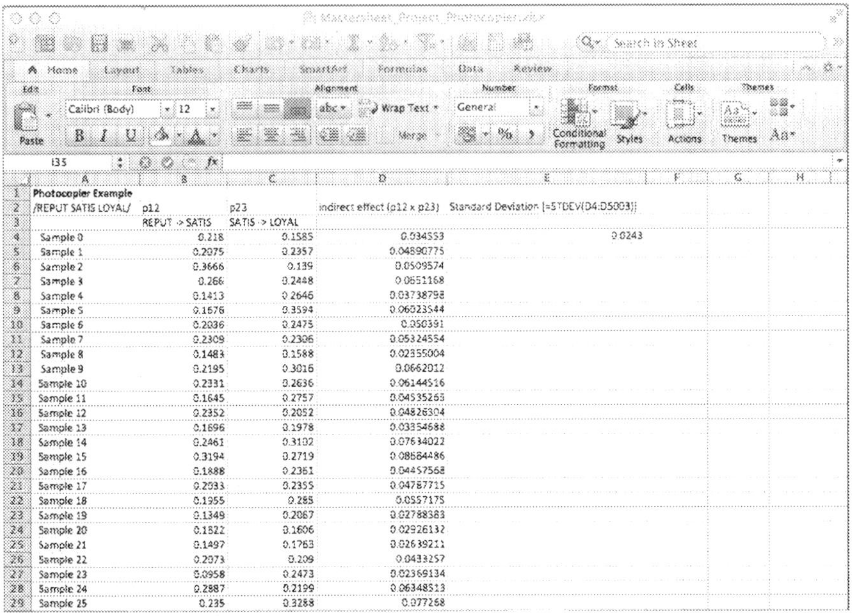

	A	B	C	D	E
1	**Photocopier Example**				
2	/REPUT SATIS LOYAL/	p12	p23	indirect effect (p12 x p23)	Standard Deviation [=STDEV(D4:D5003)]
3		REPUT -> SATIS	SATIS -> LOYAL		
4	Sample 0	0.218	0.1585	0.034553	0.0243
5	Sample 1	0.2075	0.2357	0.04890775	
6	Sample 2	0.3666	0.139	0.0509574	
7	Sample 3	0.266	0.2448	0.0651168	
8	Sample 4	0.1413	0.2646	0.03738798	
9	Sample 5	0.1676	0.3594	0.06023544	
10	Sample 6	0.2036	0.2475	0.050391	
11	Sample 7	0.2309	0.2306	0.05324554	
12	Sample 8	0.1483	0.1588	0.02355004	
13	Sample 9	0.2195	0.3016	0.0662012	
14	Sample 10	0.2331	0.2636	0.06144516	
15	Sample 11	0.1645	0.2757	0.04535265	
16	Sample 12	0.2352	0.2052	0.04826304	
17	Sample 13	0.1696	0.1978	0.03354688	
18	Sample 14	0.2461	0.3102	0.07634022	
19	Sample 15	0.3194	0.2719	0.08684486	
20	Sample 16	0.1888	0.2361	0.04457568	
21	Sample 17	0.2033	0.2355	0.04787715	
22	Sample 18	0.1955	0.285	0.0557175	
23	Sample 19	0.1349	0.2067	0.02788383	
24	Sample 20	0.1822	0.1606	0.02926132	
25	Sample 21	0.1497	0.1763	0.02639211	
26	Sample 22	0.2073	0.209	0.0433257	
27	Sample 23	0.0958	0.2473	0.02369134	
28	Sample 24	0.2887	0.2199	0.06348513	
29	Sample 25	0.235	0.3288	0.077268	

Magnitude of Mediation

Once the significance of the indirect effect is established, the strength of the mediator can be examined through the use of total effect[103] and variance account for (VAF)[104]. Mediation analysis results are presented in Figure 96. It can be said that only 8.9% of REPUT's effect on LOYAL can be explained via the SATIS mediator. Since the VAF is smaller than the 20% threshold level, SATIS is argued to have no mediating effect[105] on the REPUT→LOYAL linkage. However, 21.3% of PRICE's effect on LOYAL can be explained via the SATIS mediator and the magnitude is

[103] Total effect = direct effect + indirect effect. For example, in H_6, the total effect is 0.505 + 0.049 = 0.554.

[104] VAF = indirect effect/total effect. For example, again in H_6, VAF = 0.049/0.554 = 0.089.

[105] According to Hair et al. (2013), partial mediation is demonstrated when VAF exceeds the 0.2 threshold level and that full mediation is demonstrated when it exceeds 0.8.

considered to be partial. These findings lead us to reject hypothesis H_7 but accept hypothesis H_8 about SATIS's mediator role.

Figure 96: Mediation Analysis in PLS-SEM

Hypothesis	Procedure	Path:	Path Coef.	Indirect Effect	STDEV	Total Effect	VAF	*t* Values	Sig. Levels	*p* Values	Hypothesis
H6	Step 1: Direct effect (without mediator)	REPUT --> LOYAL	0.550	n/a				13.931	***	0.000	Rejected
	Step 2: Indirect Effect (with mediator)	REPUT --> LOYAL	0.505	n/a		0.554	0.089				
		REPUT --> SATIS	0.220	0.049	0.024						
		SATIS --> LOYAL	0.224					2.029	**	0.050	
H7	Step 1: Direct Effect (without mediator)	PRICE --> LOYAL	0.473	n/a				11.269	***	0.000	Accepted
	Step 2: Indirect Effect (with mediator)	PRICE --> LOYAL	0.369	n/a		0.469	0.213				
		PRICE --> SATIS	0.445	0.100	0.038						
		SATIS --> LOYAL	0.224					2.645	***	0.010	

CHAPTER 11

Comparing Groups Using Categorical Moderation Analysis (PLS-MGA)

Multi-group Analysis – "Business Type" in the Photocopier Manufacturer Example

Before starting this research project, Susan's colleagues in the sales department keep telling her that non-profit business customers often behave very differently from for-profit ones in their decision-making processes. To confirm such insights, the last hypothesis is built as follows:

H_8: *There is significant categorical moderating effect of business type on the relationship among model constructs.*

A multi-group analysis (PLS-MGA) is conducted using the parametric approach[106] as suggested by Keil et al., (2000). This way, Susan can explore if there is any categorical moderating effect of business type (i.e., non-profit = group 1; for-profit = group 2) on her research findings. This kind of concern is understandable because heterogeneity may exist to show significantly differences in model relationships. Becker, Rai, Ringle, & Völckner (2013) advise that researchers who failed to consider this potential issue may draw incorrect conclusions.

The main idea is to check if the variances of the PLS parameter estimates (i.e. path coefficients) differ significantly across the 2 groups. The

---

[106] The Keil et al. (2000) approach involves a modified two-independent-sample t test to compare path coefficient across two groups of data. With the help of bootstrapping, the standard deviation of the path coefficient can be calculated.

standard errors[107] of the PLS parameter estimates can be found using the bootstrapping procedure[108]. As revealed in Figure 97, only 1 relationship (PRICE → LOYAL) differs significantly[109] across the two groups. All other path coefficients do not differ significantly. The lack of heterogeneity leads us to reject the eighth hypothesis (H_8) about the categorical moderation role of business type in the model.

Figure 97: Results of Multi-group Analysis (PLS-MGA)

Hypothesis		Group 1: Non-profit		Group 2: For-profit		Group 1 vs. Group 2				Hypothesis
		p1	se(p(1))	p2	se(p(2))	|p(1)-p(2)|	t Value	Significance Level	p Value	
H8	REPUT --> LOYAL	0.486	0.069	0.535	0.058	0.049	0.545	NS	0.587	Rejected
	SATIS --> LOYAL	0.241	0.084	0.195	0.085	0.046	0.386	NS	0.700	
	PRICE --> LOYAL	0.371	0.091	0.365	0.076	0.006	3.266	***	0.001	
	REPUT --> SATIS	0.147	0.108	0.307	0.108	0.160	1.050	NS	0.295	
	PRICE --> SATIS	0.470	0.131	0.416	0.122	0.054	0.300	NS	0.764	
	n		106		54						

Note: p(1) and p(2) are path coefficients of Group 1 and Group 2, respectively; se(p(1)) and se(p(2)) are the standard error of p(1) and p(2), respectively.

*p<0.10. **p<0.05. ***p<0.01 NS=not significant

Summary of Hypothesis Testing

All of the hypotheses except two are accepted in Susan's research, and their results are summarized in Figure 98. REPUT is found to have significant impact to both LOYAL and SATIS (H_1 & H_2), whereas PRICE significantly influences these two endogenous variables as well (H_3 &

---

[107] The bootstrapping standard deviation is the same as the bootstrapping standard error in SmartPLS.

[108] To find the standard error (se(p(1)) of the parameter estimates in Group 1, run bootstrap with 106 cases; to find the standard error (se(p2)) of the parameter estimates in Group 2, run bootstrap with 95 cases. See "Report → Default Report → Bootstrapping → path coefficients (Mean, STDEV, *T*-Values) → standard errors"

[109] To reject the null hypothesis of equal path coefficients (i.e., to prove that the path coefficient is different across the 2 groups), the empirical *T*-Value must be larger than the critical value from a *T* distribution with $n^1 + n^2 - 2$ degrees of freedom.

H_4). It has also been found that SATIS maintains a significant linkage to LOYAL (H_5). Meanwhile, SATIS serves as a significant mediator to the relationship between PRICE and LOYAL (H_7). There is no significant categorical moderating effect of the business type in the model so the last hypothesis (H_8) is rejected.

Figure 98: Summary of Hypothesis Testing

	Hypotheses	Accepted? (Yes/No)
H_1	Brand reputation (REPUT) significantly influences customer loyalty (LOYAL)	Yes
H_2	Brand reputation (REPUT) significantly influences customer satisfaction (SATIS)	Yes
H_3	Pricing (PRICE) significantly influences customer loyalty (LOYAL)	Yes
H_4	Pricing (PRICE) significantly influences customer satisfaction (SATIS)	Yes
H_5	Customer satisfaction (SATIS) significantly influences customer loyalty (LOYAL)	Yes
H_6	Customer satisfaction (SATIS) significantly mediates the relationship between brand reputation (REPUT) and customer loyalty (LOYAL)	No
H_7	Customer satisfaction (SATIS) significantly mediates the relationship between pricing (PRICE) and customer loyalty (LOYAL)	Yes
H_8	There is significant categorical moderating effect of business type on the relationship among model constructs	No

Managerial Implications for the Photocopier Manufacturer

This research has provided Susan with several insights into her photocopier business, especially the factors that drive loyalty from her business customers. The following findings and managerial implications can be drawn:

1. Customer loyalty is influenced by several factors, including but not limit to brand reputation, product pricing, and customer satisfaction. Resources have to be allocated to look after these areas in general.

2. Out of these three factors, brand reputation is the most important one, followed by pricing and then customer satisfaction. That means the company should make brand reputation management a priority, in case sufficient resources are not available to manage these three areas at the same time.

3. Brand reputation is not a single-dimension factor. Instead, it is mostly affected by customers' perception of the company's product/service quality and financial performance, followed by its governance and leadership performance. Resources should be allocated in this sequence if they are limited. Contrary to common belief, this research does not find corporate social responsibility to have any significant relationship with brand reputation. As such, the company should first focus on the mentioned four areas of brand reputation before increasing the company's corporate social responsibility initiatives.

4. This research shows that customer satisfaction significantly mediates the strengths between pricing and loyalty. This means that if the customers are dissatisfied, they may not become loyal to the photocopier manufacturer even if the price is reasonable. As a result, account managers should not simply focus on getting the lowest pricing for their customers; it would be more important for them to understand their customers' needs, react to their concerns, and keep them satisfied.

5. No significant categorical moderating effect of business type is observed in this research, so the same conclusion can be drawn for both non-profit and for-profit organizations. In other words, Susan does not need to run separate programs to drive customer loyalty for each of these customer segments.

CHAPTER 12

New Techniques in PLS-SEM

Estimating Factor Models Using Consistent PLS (Plsc)

The traditional PLS algorithm has its shortcomings. Dijkstra & Schermelleh-Engel (2014) argue that it overestimates the loadings in absolute value and underestimates multiple and bivariate correlations between latent variables. It is also found that the R^2 value of endogenous latent variables is often underestimated (Dijkstra, 2010).

Building on Nunnally's (1978) famous correction for attenuation formula, the Consistent PLS (PLSc) is proposed to correct reflective constructs' correlations to make estimation results consistent with a factor-model (Dijkstra 2010; Dijkstra 2014; Dijkstra and Henseler 2015a; Dijkstra and Schermelleh-Engel 2014). In SmartPLS v3, the developers have added "Consistent PLS Algorithm" and "Consistent PLS Bootstrapping" to account for the correlations among reflective factors (see Figure 99).

Figure 99. Consistent PLS Algorithm and Consistent PLS Bootstrapping

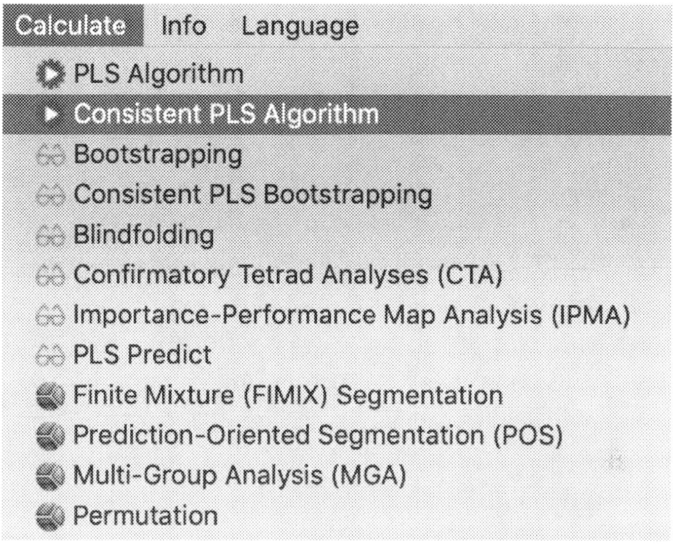

The original PLS Algorithm and Bootstrapping functions are still available in the software. Which to choose depends on whether the researcher's model has reflective or formative constructs:

- If all constructs are reflective: use Consistent PLS Algorithm and Bootstrapping
- If all constructs are formative: use PLS Algorithm and Bootstrapping (the original one)
- If there is a mixture of reflective and formative constructs: use Consistent PLS Algorithm and Bootstrapping

In other words, if the constructs are modeled as factors, the researcher should use consistent PLS (PLSc) instead of traditional PLS with Mode A. There are also other considerations when using PLSc. For example, if a researcher's model utilizes a higher-order construct, he or she should just use the two-stage approach and not the repeated indicator approach as the latter does not work well with PLSc. Also, if there is a huge discrepancy between the traditional PLS and PLSc results, the researcher should rethink if all reflective constructs truly follow a common factor model, or if they should use a composite (formative) model instead.

Assessing Discriminant Validity Using Heterotrait-Monotrait Ratio of Correlations (HTMT)

In PLS-SEM where there are reflective constructs, it is important to assess discriminant validity when analyzing relationships between latent variables. Discriminant validity needs to be established in order to confirm that the hypothesized structural paths results are real and not the result of statistical discrepancies.

The classical approach in assessing discriminant validity relies on examining (i) the Fornell-Larcker criterion, and (ii) partial cross-loadings. This information is still available in the result report of SmartPLS v3. However, Henseler, Ringle and Sarstedt (2015) argued that these approaches cannot reliably detect the lack of discriminant validity in most research scenarios. They proposed an alternative approach called Heterotrait-monotrait ratio of correlations (HTMT) which is based on the multitrait-multimethod matrix.

HTMT Procedures

1. Let us use the "cafe100" dataset to illustrate how HTMT can be performed to check discriminant validity.
2. Go to the "Calculate" menu and select "Consistent PLS Algorithm".
3. Under the "Setup" tab, check "Connect all LVs for Initial Calculation" and then press the "Start Calculation" button.
4. Once the algorithm converged, go to the "Quality Criteria" section and click the "Discriminant Validity" hyperlink.
5. Go to the 3rd tab where it says "Heterotrait-Monotrait Ratio (HTMT)" (see Figure 100).

Figure 100: Heterotrait-Monotrait Ratio of Correlations (HTMT) Values

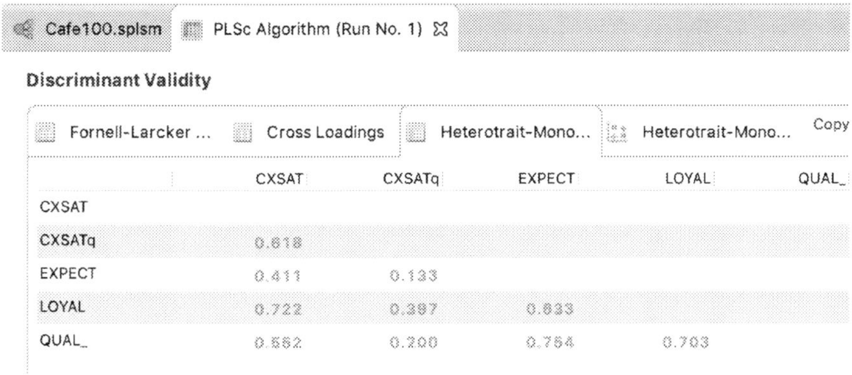

	CXSAT	CXSATq	EXPECT	LOYAL	QUAL_
CXSAT					
CXSATq	0.618				
EXPECT	0.411	0.133			
LOYAL	0.722	0.397	0.833		
QUAL_	0.582	0.200	0.754	0.703	

6. Check the values. Since the maximum value 0.754 is below the 0.85 thresholds (i.e., the most conservative HTMT value), we say that discriminant validity is established in the model.

7. The next step is to assess HTMT inference criterion. To do that, first go back to the colorful model tab. Then, go to the "Calculate" menu and select "Consistent PLS Bootstrapping".

8. On the 2nd tab "Bootstrapping", choose "Complete Bootstrapping" in the "Amount of Results" selection. This is an important step or else HTMT info will not be displayed.

9. Click the "Start Calculation" button to perform the bootstrapping procedure.

10. Once the result report opens, go to "Quality Criteria" and click the "Heterotrait-Monotrait Ratio (HTMT)" hyperlink. You may need to scroll down in order to view this link at the bottom of the screen.

11. Go to the 2nd tab "Confidence Intervals Bias Corrected" to check the values (see Figure 101).

Figure 101: Confidence Intervals of HTMT

| | Cafe100.splsm | PLSc Algorithm (Run No. 1) | Bootstrapping (c) (Run No. 1) |

Heterotrait-Monotrait Ratio (HTMT)

| | Confidence Intervals | Confidence Intervals Bias Corrected | Samples | Copy |

	Original Sample (C	Sample Mean (M)	Bias	2.5%	97.5%
EXPECT -> CXSAT	0.411	0.414	0.002	0.238	0.568
LOYAL -> CXSAT	0.722	0.725	0.002	0.602	0.837
LOYAL -> EXPECT	0.633	0.631	-0.002	0.467	0.782
QUAL_ -> CXSAT	0.552	0.545	-0.007	0.388	0.691
QUAL_ -> EXPECT	0.754	0.755	0.001	0.569	0.892
QUAL_ -> LOYAL	0.703	0.701	-0.002	0.542	0.808

12. Look at the CI low (2.5%) and CI Up (97.5%) columns. Since all HTMT are significantly different from 1, discriminant validity is said to be established between these reflective constructs.

Contrasting Total Effects Using Importance-Performance Matrix Analysis (IPMA)

SmartPLS v3 has introduced a new way of reporting PLS-SEM results — The importance-performance matrix analysis (IPMA). It is often used in evaluating the performance of key business success drivers. IPMA is basically a xy-plot where the x-axis shows the "Importance" (Total Effect) of business success drivers using a scale of 0 to 1, and the y-axis shows the "Performance" of business success drivers using a scale of 0 to 100. This way, researchers can identify those predecessor constructs that have a strong total effect (high importance) but low average latent variable scores (low performance) for subsequent operational improvement.

IPMA requires the use of a metric scale or equidistant scale (with balanced positive and negative categories with a neutral category in the middle). Hence, indicators being measured on a nominal scale cannot utilize IPMA.

IPMA Procedures

1. Let us use the "cafe100" dataset to illustrate IPMA.
2. Run PLS Algorithm by going to the "Calculate" menu and select "Consistent PLS Algorithm"
3. On the Results Report, check the signs of the outer weight to see if they are positive or negative by going to "Final Results → Outer Weights". In general, we want positive values. If there are any indicators having negative values (e.g., those larger than-0.1), they should be removed prior to running IPMA. In our case, all values are positive (see Figure 102), so we can proceed with IPMA.

Figure 102: Outer Weight

Outer Weights

	CXSAT	CXSATq	EXPECT	LOYAL	QUAL_
expect_1			0.485		
expect_2			0.346		
expect_3			0.271		
expect_4			0.208		
loyal_1				0.298	
loyal_2				0.302	
loyal_3				0.305	
loyal_4				0.258	
qual_1					0.338
qual_2					0.261
qual_3					0.269
qual_4					0.292

4. Go back to the colorful model tab, then select "Importance-Performance Map Analysis (IPMA)" in the "Calculate" menu.
5. Specify the target construct LOYAL in the "Setup" tab, and choose the "All Predecessors of the Selected Target Construct" option. Also, enter the min or max value of the scale and press the "Apply

to All" button. Once it's all done, press the "Start Calculation" button (see Figure 103).

Figure 103: IPMA Setup

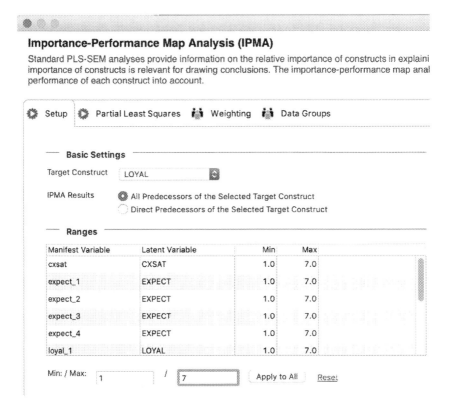

6. To view IPMA result graphically, go to "Quality Criteria → Importance-Performance Map [LOYAL] (constructs, unstandardized effects)" on the Results Page (see Figure 104).

Figure 104: IPMA Results

7. As shown in Figure 104, QUAL has a high total effect (i.e., high importance) but low performance in driving customer loyalty, so this is an area that the café owner should not be ignored for improvement once she has addressed the EXPECT items.

Testing Goodness of Model Fit (GoF) Using SRMR, d_{ULS}, and d_G

Prior to the development of Consistent PLS (PLSc), there was an established view that PLS-SEM could not be assessed globally for the overall model because it did not optimize any global scalar function (Henseler, Hubona and Ray, 2016). For years, it has been argued that the overall goodness-of-fit (GoF) cannot reliably distinguish valid from invalid models in PLS-SEM so this kind of assessment is rarely used and reported.

However, testing GoF as a way to contrast models is now possible under PLSc since it is a full-blown SEM method that provides consistent estimates for both factor and composite models. Researchers can now assess GoF within PLSc to determine whether a model is well-fitted or ill-fitted (Henseler et al, 2014), and to detect measurement model misspecification and structural model misspecification (Dijkstra and Henseler, 2014). Specifically, we want to understand the discrepancy between the "observed"[110] or "approximated"[111] values of the dependent variables and the values predicted by the PLS model.

There are 3 different approaches to assess the model's goodness-of-fit (Henseler et al, 2016):

(i) Approximate fit criterion: **The standardized root mean squared residual (SRMR)**[112]

The lower the SRMR, the better the model's fit. Perfect fit is obtained when SRMR is zero. SRMR value of 0.08 or lower is acceptable. A value significantly larger than 0.08 suggests the absence of fit.[113]

(ii) Exact fit criterion: **The unweighted least squares discrepancy (d_{ULS})**[114]

The lower the d_{ULS}, the better the model's fit.

(iii) Exact fit criterion: **The geodesic discrepancy (d_G)**[115]

The lower the d_G, the better the model's fit.

GoF Procedures

1. Let us use the "cafe100" dataset to illustrate how GoF can be assessed.
2. Go to the "Calculate" menu and select "Consistent PLS Algorithm".
3. Under the "Setup" tab, check "Connect all LVs for Initial Calculation" and then press the "Start Calculation" button.
4. Once the algorithm converged, go to the "Quality Criteria" section and click the "Model Fit" hyperlink. The result is displayed in Figure 105.

---

[110] As in manifest variables

[111] As in latent variables

[112] See Hu and Bentler (1998 and 1999) for more information on SRMR

[113] See Henseler et al. (2014) for more information on acceptable SRMR values.

[114] See Dijkstra & Henseler (2015b) for more information on d_{ULS}

[115] See Dijkstra & Henseler (2015b) for more information on d_G

Figure 105: Model Fit

Model_Fit

Fit Summary		
	Saturated Model	Estimated Model
SRMR	0.085	0.086
d_ULS	0.663	0.667
d_G	0.431	0.437
Chi-Square	210.452	210.003
NFI	0.750	0.751

5. Under the "Estimated Model" column, you can now find the values for SRMR, d_{ULS}, and d_G for assessment using the guidelines as shown earlier in this section. In our model, we have an SRMR value of 0.086, which is slightly above the 0.08 threshold; this suggests a poor theoretical model fit.

CHAPTER 13

Recommended PLS-SEM Resources

Books

Handbook of Partial Least Squares (PLS) and Marketing: Concepts, Methods, and Applications
Editors: Vincenzo Esposito Vinzi, Wynne W. Chin, Jörg Henseler, & Huiwen Wangalso
Publisher: Springer, 2010

Partial Least Squares Structural Equation Modeling: Basic Concepts, Methodological Issues and Applications
Editors: Latan, H., & Noonan, R.
Publisher: Springer, 2017

A Primer on Partial Least Squares Structural Equation Modeling (PLS-SEM)
Authors: Joseph F. Hair, Jr., G. Tomas M. Hult, Christian Ringle, and Marko Sarstedt
Publisher: Sage, 2017

Partial Least Squares Structural Equation Modeling: Recent Advances in Banking and Finance
Editors: Avkiran, N. K., & Ringle, C. M.
Publisher: Springer, 2018

Conferences

International Conference on Partial Least Squares and Related Methods

Every few years, professors around the world come together to present their insights on PLS-SEM. Often, many useful papers and PowerPoint presentations from the presenters can be downloaded from the conference website. The International Conference on Partial Least Squares and Related Methods has been held in the following years and locations:

> PLS'99 in Jouy-en-Josas (France)
> PLS'01 in Anacapri (Italy)
> PLS'03 in Lisbon (Portugal)
> PLS'05 in Barcelona (Spain)
> PLS'07 in Ås (Norway)
> PLS'09 in Beijing (China)
> PLS'12 in Houston (USA)
> PLS'14 in Paris (France) Web: https://sites.google.com/site/partialleastsquares2014/
> PLS'17 in Macau (China) Web: https://www.aconf.org/conf_86922.html

Discussion Forums

The PLS-SEM Forum on Google Groups
Web: https://groups.google.com/forum/#!forum/pls-sem

SmartPLS' Discussion Forum
Web: http://forum.smartpls.com

ResearchGate
Web: http://www.researchgate.net
Note: ResearchGate does not officially run any forums but there is a great "search" function where you can locate Q&A on any topics related to PLS-SEM.

Training Workshops

PLS School workshop
Web: http://www.pls-school.com
Contact: Dr. Jörg Henseler (University of Twente, Enschede)

PLS-SEMINARS
Web: https://www.udemy.com/user/drgeoffreyhubona/
Contact: Dr. Geoffrey Hubona (Texas A&M International University)

PLS-SEM Courses
Web: https://www.pls-sem.net/courses
Contact: Dr. Joseph F. Hair (University of Southern Alabama), Dr. Christian M. Ringle (Hamburg University of Tech), and Dr. Marko Sarstedt (OVGU Magdeburg)

Software

ADANCO
Platform: Windows
Version: 2.1.0
Web: https://www.composite-modeling.com
Developers: Prof. Dr. Jörg Henseler and Prof. Dr. Theo K. Dijkstra
Note: This software can model composites, common factors, and single-indicator constructs. It also facilitates causal and predictive modeling.

Desktop PLS-GUI Application
Version: Beta December 2014
Web: https://pls-gui.com
Developers: Prof. Geoffrey Hubona and Dean Lim
Note: This software is still in beta version.

PLS-Graph
Platform: Windows
Version: 3.0
Developer: Soft Modeling, Inc. / Prof. Wynne W. Chin
Web: http://www.plsgraph.com/

Mastering

Download: Not publicly available.
Price: Free, subject to author's approval
Note: Development of this software has been discontinued.

plspm
Platform: Windows and MacOSX
Version: 0.4.9
Download: http://cran.r-project.org/web/packages/plspm/index.html
Price: Free
Note: This software requires the use of "r" Statistical Software

SmartPLS
Platform: Windows and Mac OSX
Version: 2.0M3 (Windows only) and 3.2.8 (Windows and Mac)
Web: http://www.smartpls.com
Price: Free for v2; Free and paid versions for v3

VisualPLS
Platform: Windows
Version: 1.04b1
Developer: Professor Jen-Ruei Fu
Web: http://www2.kuas.edu.tw/prof/fred/vpls/index.html
Download: https://www.openfoundry.org/of/projects/604/download
Price: Free
Note: Development of this software has been discontinued.

WarpPLS
Platform: Windows
Version: 6.0
Developer: ScriptWarp Systems / Dr. Ned Kock
Web: http://www.scriptwarp.com/warppls
Download: http://download.cnet.com/WarpPLS/3000-20411_4-75042779.html
Note: Time-limited fully functional free trial available; commercial version available.

XLSTAT-PLSPM/Marketing/Psy/Premium
Platform: Windows and Mac OSX
Developer: XLSTAT
Web: http://www.xlstat.com/en/products/xlstat-plspm/
Note: This software requires the use of Microsoft Excel

Others

- Older software packages include DOS-based LVPLS 1.8 (Jan-Bernd Lohmöller's and Yuen Li's versions) and PLS-GUI 2.01. However, they are no longer available for download and their software developments have been discontinued.
- PLS procedure/module is available for SAS and Coheris SPAD.
- IBM's SPSS (since version 17) supports limited PLS function (regression but not path modeling) using a free third-party Python plug-in that can be downloaded from SPSS's Developer Central site (http://www.ibm.com/developerworks/spssdevcentral). The path is "Resources → IBM SPSS Statistics → Tools and Utilities → Statistical Tools → PLS.spe" A pre-requisite is to have the appropriate version of the Python plugin or Python Essentials installed on your computer, plus the "numpy" and "scipy" Python libraries. You can also download these Python plugin and Python Essentials files in the above site, under the "Tools and Utilities" section.

Reference Journal Papers

There are many great journal articles on PLS-SEM, please refer to the "References" section at the end of this book for a full list of publications. If you want to see how PLS-SEM can be applied in retail research, you can have a good read of the following article that was published in a tier-1 journal. I wrote it together with Professor Osmud Rahman and Professor Hong Yu when I was teaching at Ryerson University:

Rahman, O., Wong, K.K., and Yu, H., (2016) The effects of mall personality and fashion orientation on shopping value and mall patronage intention.

Journal of Retailing and Consumer Services, 28 (1), 155-164. doi:10.1016/j.
jretconser.2015.09.008

The field of PLS-SEM has advanced significantly in recent years with new
insights and guidelines from scholars. The following journal article, written
by Professor Dr. Jörg Henseler, Professor Geoffrey Hubona, and Professor
Pauline Ash Ray, is a great one that summarizes the modern view on PLS
path modeling as compared to the traditional ones:

Hensler, J., Hubona, G., & Ray, P.-A. (2016). Using PLS path modeling
in new technology research: updated guidelines. *Industrial Management
& Data Systems*, 116(1), 2-20.

Finally, it is important to remember that there is no "perfect" statistical
method on this planet that can handle all kinds of research designs and
data. PLS, as an emerging variance-based SEM method, certainly has
its strengths and weaknesses. Unlike those CB-SEM methods that have
been used widely for decades, PLS-SEM is still relatively new to many
researchers and it is not uncommon to see scholars hold different views on
this research method. In fact, constructive criticism and debates are great
ways to advance a new research method to the next level through better
understanding of its capabilities and limitations. Readers are encouraged
to review the following article written by Professor Mikko Rönkkö and
Professor Joerg Evermann who criticized PLS-SEM, and the rejoinder
provided Professor Dr. Jörg Henseler and his team:

Rönkkö, M., Evermann, J. (2013). A critical examination of common
beliefs about partial least squares path modeling. *Organizational Research
Methods*, 16(3), 425–448. DOI:10.1177/1094428112474693

Henseler, J., Dijkstra, T. K., Sarstedt, M., Ringle, C. M., Diamantopoulos,
A., Straub, D. W., ... Calantone, R. J. (2014). Common Beliefs and Reality
About PLS: Comments on Ronnkko and Evermann (2013). *Organizational
Research Methods*, 17(2), 182-209. DOI:10.1177/1094428114526928

CONCLUSION

PLS-SEM is an emerging statistical procedure for structural modeling that researchers can consider when conducting research projects with a limited number of participants. This book helps readers to understand how PLS-SEM can be applied in both B2C and B2B marketing researches through the use of some fictitious examples. Although PLS-SEM seems to be a silver bullet for tackling dataset with small sample size and non-normal data distribution, researchers must not ignore the proper model assessments prior to drawing a conclusion. There are many aspects of this statistical procedure such as reliability, validity, collinearity issues, predictive relevance, and effect sizes that have to be assessed, in addition to reporting the coefficient of determination and path coefficients as found in the model.

PLS-SEM can be easily configured to perform advanced modeling such as mediation, categorical moderation, and higher-order construct analysis so it can be a powerful research tool to academics and practitioners. Finally, the PLS-SEM community has come together to advance this statistical methodology through intensive debates about its strengths and weaknesses. Whether you hold a traditional or modern view of PLS, there is no doubt that this methodology will continue to evolve and play a key role in today's business research.

EPILOGUE

Life after PLS-SEM?

The proliferation of PLS-SEM has inspired many academics to explore innovative ways of analyzing data. PLS has laid the foundation for the development of newer statistical procedures such as generalized structured component analysis (GSCA), championed by Dr. Heungsun Hwang of McGill University (www.sem-gesca.org). Originally developed as a stand-alone Windows application called VisualGSCA, GeSCA is now available as a free web-based tool. It is well known for its ability to deal with missing observations, handle second-order latent variables, and generate overall measures of model fit. Another new development is universal structural modelling (USM), developed by Dr. Frank Buckler of NEUSREL Causal Analytics (www.neusrel.com). USM is implemented through the NEUSREL software, which is based on MathWorks' MATLAB and Microsoft's Excel software. It is well known for its ability to model nonlinearities, interactions and paths. Since GSCA and USM are still relatively new as compared to CB-SEM and PLS-SEM, readers are advised to exercise caution in their use of these approaches and tools. As the case of PLS-SEM has demonstrated, any new statistical technique has its limitations; hence, it must go through extensive critical reviews and examinations prior to gaining acceptance in the research community.

REFERENCES

Albers, S. (2010). PLS and success factor studies in marketing. In V. Esposito Vinzi, W. W. Chin, J. Henseler, & H. Wang (Eds.), *Handbook of partial least squares: Concepts, methods, and applications in marketing and related fields* (pp. 409-425). Berlin, Heidelberg: Springer.

Bacon, L. D. (1999). Using LISREL and PLS to Measure Customer Satisfaction, *Sawtooth Software Conference Proceedings*, La Jolla, California, Feb 2-5, 305-306.

Bagozzi, R. P., & Yi, Y. (1988). On the evaluation of structural equation models. *Journal of the Academy of Marketing Science*, 16(1), 74–94.

Bass, B., Avolio, B., Jung, D., & Berson Y. (2003). Predicting unit performance by assessing transformational and transactional leadership. *Journal of Applied Psychology* 88(2), 207–218.

Becker, J. M., Rai, A. Ringle, C. M. & Völckner, F. (2013). Discovering unobserved heterogeneity in structural equation models to avert validity threats. *MIS Quarterly 37*(3), 665-694.

Biong, H., & Ulvnes, A.M. (2011). If the supplier's human capital walks away, where would the customer go? *Journal of Business-to-Business Marketing*, 18(3), 223-252.

Bollen, K. A. (2011). Evaluating effect, composite, and causal indicators in structural equation models. *MIS Quarterly*, 35(2), 359-372.

Bollen, K. A., & Bauldry, S. (2011). Three Cs in measurement models: Causal indicators, composite indicators, and covariates. *Psychological Methods*, 16(3), 265-284.

Carrion, G. C. Henseler, J., Ringle, C.M., & Roldan, J.L. (2016). Prediction-oriented modeling in business research by means of PLS path modeling: Introduction to a JBR special section. *Journal of Business Research*, 69(10), 4545-4551.

Chin, W. W. (1998). The partial least squares approach to structural equation modeling. In G. A. Marcoulides (Ed.), *Modern methods for business research* (295–336). Mahwah, New Jersey: Lawrence Erlbaum Associates.

Chin, W.W., & Dibbern, J. (2010) An Introduction to a Permutation Based Procedure for Multi-Group PLS Analysis: Results of Tests of Differences on Simulated Data and a Cross Cultural Analysis of the Sourcing of Information System Services Between Germany and the USA. In V. Esposito Vinzi, W. W. Chin, J. Henseler, & H. Wang (Eds.), *Handbook of partial least squares: Concepts, methods, and applications in marketing and related fields* (pp. 171-193). Berlin, Heidelberg: Springer.

Chin, W. W., Marcolin, B. L., & Newsted, P. R. (1996). *A partial least squares latent variable modelling approach for measuring interaction effects: Results from a Monte Carlo simulation study and voice mail emotion/adoption study.* Paper presented at the 17th International Conference on Information Systems, Cleveland, OH.

Chin, W. W., Marcolin, B. L., & Newsted, P. R (2003). "A Partial Least Squares Latent Variable Modeling Approach For Measuring Interaction Effects: Results From A Monte Carlo Simulation Study And Electronic Mail Emotion/Adoption Study", *Information Systems Research*, 14(2), 189-217.

Cohen, J. (1988). *Statistical power analysis for the behavioural sciences.* Mahwah, NJ: Lawrence Erlbaum.

Cohen, J. (1992). A power primer. *Psychological Bulletin*, 112(1), 155-159.

Diamantopoulos, A., Sarstedt, M. Fuchs, C., Kaiser, S., & Wilczynski, P. (2012). Guidelines for choosing between multi-item and single-item scales for construct measurement: A predictive validity perspective. *Journal of the Academy of Marketing Science*, 40, 434–449.

Dijkstra, T. K. (2010). Latent Variables and Indices: Herman Wold's Basic Design and Partial Least Squares. In. V. Esposito Vinzi, W.W. Chin, J. Henseler & H. Wang (Eds) *Handbook of Partial Least Squares: Concepts, Methods and Applications* (p23-46). Berlin, Germany: Springer Berlin Heidelberg. DOI: 10.1007/978-3-540-32827-8_2

Dijkstra, T. K. (2014). PLS' Janus Face – Response to Professor Rigdon's 'Rethinking Partial Least Squares Modeling: In Praise of Simple Methods', *Long Range Planning*, 47(3), 146-153.

Dijkstra, T. K., & Henseler, J. (2014). Assessing and testing the goodness-of-fit of PLS path models, *3rd VOC Conference*, Leiden, May 9.

Dijkstra, T. K., & Henseler, J. (2015a). Consistent Partial Least Squares Path Modeling, *MIS Quarterly*, 39(2): 297-316.

Dijkstra, T. K., & Henseler, J. (2015b). Consistent and asymptotically normal PLS estimators for linear structural equations. *Computational Statistics & Data Analysis,81*(1), 10–23.

Dijkstra, T. K., & Schermelleh-Engel, K. (2014). Consistent partial least squares for nonlinear structural equation models. *Psychometrika*, 79(4), 585-604.

Eisenbeiss, M., Cornelißen, M., Backhaus, K., & Hoyer, W. D. (2014). Nonlinear and asymmetric returns on customer satisfaction: Do they vary across situations and consumers? *Journal of the Academy of Marketing Science*, *42*(3), 242-263.

Ernst, M. D. (2004). Permutation methods: A basis for exact inference. *Statistical Science*, 19(4), 676-685.

Esposito Vinzi V., Trinchera L., Squillacciotti S., Tenenhaus M. (2008). REBUS-PLS: A response-based procedure for detecting unit segments in PLS path modeling, *Applied Stochastic Models in Business and Industry (ASMBI)*, 24(5), 439-458.

Esposito Vinzi, V., Trinchera, L., & Amato, S. (2010). PLS Path Modeling: From Foundations to Recent Developments and Open Issues for Model Assessment and Improvement. In. V. Esposito Vinzi, W.W. Chin, J. Henseler & H. Wang (Eds) *Handbook of Partial Least Squares: Concepts, Methods and Applications* (47-82) Berlin, Germany: Springer Berlin Heidelberg

Fornell, C., & Larcker, D.F., (1981). Evaluating structural equation models with unobservable variables and measurement error. *Journal of Marketing Research*, 18(1), 39-50.

Frank, B. & Hennig-Thurau, T. (2008). 'Identifying Hidden Structures in Marketing's Structural Models Through Universal Structure Modeling: An Explorative Bayesian Neural Network Complement to LISREL and PLS', *Marketing--Journal of Research and Management*, 4(2), 47-66.

Garver, M. S., & Mentzer, J.T. (1999). Logistics research methods: Employing structural equation modeling to test for construct validity. *Journal of Business Logistics*, *20*(1), 33–57.

Good, P. (2000). *Permutation tests: A practical guide to resampling methods for testing hypotheses*. New York, NY: Springer.

Gudergan, S. P., Ringle, C. M., Wende, S., and Will, A. (2008). Confirmatory Tetrad Analysis in PLS Path Modeling, *Journal of Business Research*, 61(12), 1238-1249.

Haenlein, M. & Kaplan, A. M. (2004). A Beginner's Guide to Partial Least Squares Analysis, *Understanding Statistics*, 3(4), 283–297.

Hair, J. F., Black, W. C., Babin, B. J., & Anderson, R. E. (2010). *Multivariate data analysis (7ʰ ed.)*. Englewood Cliffs: Prentice Hall.

Hair, J. F., Hult, G. T. M., Ringle, C. M., & Sarstedt, M. (2013). *A Primer on Partial Least Squares Structural Equation Modeling (PLS-SEM)*. Thousand Oaks: Sage.

Hair, J. F., Ringle, C. M., & Sarstedt, M. (2011). PLS-SEM: indeed a silver bullet. *Journal of Marketing Theory and Practice*, 19(2), 139–151.

Hair, J.F., Sarstedt, M., Matthews, L., & Ringle, C.M. (2016). Identifying and Treating Unobserved Heterogeneity with FIMIX-PLS: Part I-Method, *European Business Review*, 28(1), 63-76.

Hair, J. F., Sarstedt, M., Pieper, T. & Ringle, C.M. (2012). The use of partial least squares structural equation modeling in strategic management research: A review of past practices and recommendations for future applications. *Long Range Planning*, 45(5/6), 320-340.

Hair, J.F., Sarstedt, M., Ringle, C.M. & Mena, J.A., (2012). An Assessment of the Use of Partial Least Squares Structural Equation Modeling in Marketing Research. *Journal of the Academy of Marketing Science*, 40(3), 414-433.

Hay, D. A. & Morris, D. J. (1991). *Industrial Economics and Organization: Theory and Evidence* (2ⁿᵈ ed). Oxford University Press: New York.

Henseler, J. (2010). On the convergence of the partial least squares path modeling algorithm. *Computational Statistics*, 25(1), 107–120.

Henseler, J. & Dijkstra, T.K. (2015). "ADANCO 2.0", Composite Modeling, Kleve, available at: www.composite-modeling.com

Henseler, J., Hubona, G., & Ray, P.-A. (2016). Using PLS path modeling in new technology research: updated guidelines. *Industrial Management & Data Systems*, 116(1), 2-20.

Henseler, J., Ringle, C. M., & Sarstedt, M. (2015). A New Criterion for Assessing Discriminant Validity in Variance-based Structural Equation Modeling., *Journal of the Academy of Marketing Science*, 43(1), 115-135.

Henseler, J., Ringle, C. M., & Sarstedt, M. (2016). Testing measurement invariance of composites using partial least squares. *International Marketing Review*, 33(3), 405-431.

Henseler, J., Ringle, C., & Sinkovics, R. (2009). The use of partial least squares path modeling in international marketing. in: Sinkovics, R. R. / Ghauri, P. N. (eds.), *Advances in International Marketing*, 20, 277–320.

Henseler. J. and Sarstedt, M. (2013). Goodness-of-fit indices for partial least squares path modeling. *Computational Statistics*. 28 (2), 565-580.

Henseler, J., Dijkstra, T. K., Sarstedt, M., Ringle, C. M., Diamantopoulos, A., Straub, D. W., ... Calantone, R. J. (2014). Common Beliefs and Reality About PLS: Comments on Ronnkko and Evermann (2013). *Organizational Research Methods*, 17(2), 182-209. DOI:10.1177/1094428114526928

Hoelter, D. R. (1983). The analysis of covariance structures: Goodness-of-fit indices, *Sociological Methods and Research*, 11, 325–344.

Hoyle, R. H. (ed.) (1995). *Structural Equation Modeling*. Thousand Oaks, CA.: SAGE Publications, Inc.

Hsu, H.M., Chang, I. C., & Lai, T. W. (2016). Physician's perspectives of adopting computer-assisted navigation in orthopedic surgery. *International Journal of Medical Informatics*, 94, 207-214.

Hulland, J. (1999). Use of partial least squares (PLS) in strategic management research: a review of four recent studies. *Strategic Management Journal*, 20(2), 195–204.

Hult, G. T. M., Ketchen, D. J., Griffith, D. A., Finnegan, C. A., Gonzalez-Padron, T., Harmancioglu, N., Huang, Y., Talay, M. B., & Cavusgil, S. T. (2008). Data equivalence in cross-cultural international business research: Assessment and guidelines. *Journal of International Business Studies*, 39(6), 1027-1044.

Hwang, H., Malhotra, N. K., Kim, Y., Tomiuk, M. A., & Hong, S. (2010). A comparative study on parameter recovery of three approaches to structural equation modeling. *Journal of Marketing Research*, 47 (Aug), 699-712.

Jedidi, K., Jagpal, H. S., & DeSarbo, W. S. (1997). Finite-Mixture Structural Equation Models for Response-Based Segmentation and Unobserved Heterogeneity, *Marketing Science*, 16(1), 39-59.

Jisha, P. R., & Thomas, I. (2016). Quality of life and infertility: Influence of gender, years of martial life, resilience, and anxiety. *Psychological Studies*, 61(3), 159-169.

Jöreskog, K. G., (1973). A General Method for Estimating a Linear Structural Equation System, In A. S. Goldberger and O. D. Duncan, eds., *Structural Equation Models in the Social Sciences*, (pp.85-112), New York: Academic Press.

Kansky R., Kidd, M. & Knight, A. T. (2016). A wildlife tolerance model and case study for understanding human wildlife conflicts. *Biological Conservation*, 201, 137-145.

Keil, M. Saarinen, T., Tan, B. C. Y., Tuunainen, V., Wassenaar, A., & Wei, K.-K. (2000). A cross-cultural study on escalation of commitment behaviour in software projects. *MIS Quarterly*, 24(2), 299-325.

Lohmöller, J.B. (1989). *Latent variable path modeling with partial least squares*. Heidlberg, Germany: Physica.

Marcoulides, G. A., & Saunders, C. (2006, June). Editor's Comments – PLS: A Silver Bullet? *MIS Quarterly*, 30(2), iii-ix.

Muthén, B. O. (1989). Latent variable modeling in heterogeneous populations. *Psychometrika*, 54(4), 557-585.

Nunnally, J. C. (1978). Psychometric Theory, McGraw Hill: New York.

Nunnally, J. C., & Bernstein, I. H. (1994). *Psychometric theory* (3rd ed.). New York: McGraw-Hill.

Petter, S., Straub, D., and Rai, A. (2007). "Specifying Formative Constructs in Information Systems Research," *MIS Quarterly*, Vol. 31, No. 4, 623-656.

Rahman, O., Wong, K.K., and Yu, H., (2016) The effects of mall personality and fashion orientation on shopping value and mall patronage intention. *Journal of Retailing and Consumer Services*, 28(1), 155-164.

Reinartz, Werner J., Michael Haenlein, and Jörg Henseler (2009), "An Empirical Comparison of the Efficacy of Covariance-Based and Variance-Based SEM," *International Journal of Market Research*, 26 (4), 332–344.

Rigdon, E. E. (2014). Rethinking partial least squares path modeling: Breaking chains and forging ahead. *Long Range Planning*, 47(3), 161-167.

Ringle, C. M., & Sarstedt, M. (2016). Gain more insights from your PLS-SEM result: The importance-performance map analysis. *Industrial Management & Data Systems*, 116(9), 1865-1886.

Ringle, C. M., Wende, S., & Becker, J.-M. (2015). SmartPLS 3.0 [computer software]. GmbH: Boenningstedt. Retrieved from http://www.smartpls.com.

Ringle, C., Wende, S., & Will, A. (2005). SmartPLS 2.0 (Beta). Hamburg, (www.smartpls.de).

Rönkkö, M., Evermann, J. (2013). A critical examination of common beliefs about partial least squares path modeling. *Organizational Research Methods*, 16(3), 425–448. DOI:10.1177/1094428112474693

Sarstedt, M., Becker, J. M., Ringle, C. M. & Schwaiger, M. (2011) Uncovering and Treating Unobserved Heterogeneity with FIMIX-PLS: Which Model Selection Criterion Provides an Appropriate Number of Segments? *Schmalenbach Business Review*, 63(1), 34-62.

Sarstedt, M., Hair, J. F., Ringle, C. M., Thiele, K. O., Gudergan, S. P. (2016). Estimation Issues with PLS and CBSEM: Where the Bias Lies!, *Journal of Business Research*, 69(10), 3998-4010.

Sarstedt, M., Henseler, J., & Ringle, C. M. (2011). Multi-group analysis in partial least square (PLS) path modeling: Alternative methods and empirical results. *Advances in International Marketing*, 22, 195-218.

Sarstedt, M., & Mooi, E. A. (2014). *A concise guide to market research. The process, data, and methods using IBM SPSS statistics (2nd ed.)*. Berlin, Germany: Springer.

Sarstedt, M., Schwaiger, M., and Ringle, C. M. (2009). Do We Fully Understand the Critical Success Factors of Customer Satisfaction with Industrial Goods?-Extending Festge and Schwaiger's Model to Account for Unobserved Heterogeneity, *Journal of Business Market Management*, 3(3): 185-206.

Sosik J J, Kahai S S, Piovoso M J (2009) *Emerald Management Reviews: Group & Organization Management*, Silver bullet or voodoo statistics?

A primer for using the partial least squares data analytic technique in group and organization research. 34(1), 5-36.

Statsoft (2013). Structural Equation Modeling, Statsoft Electronic Statistics Textbook. http://www.statsoft.com/textbook/structural-equation-modeling/

Thompson, R. L., Barclay, D. & Higgins, C. (1995). "The Partial Least Squares Approach to Casual Modeling: Personal Computer Adoption and Use as an Illustration". Technogogy Studies: Special Issue on *Research Methodology, 2*(2), 285–324.

Werts, C. E., Linn, R. L., & Joreskog, K. G. (1974). Quantifying unmeasured variables. In H. M. Blalock, Jr. (Ed.), *Measurement in the Social Sciences*, Chicago: Aldine Publishing Co., 270-292.

Wold, H. (1973). Nonlinear Iterative Partial Least Squares (NIPALS) Modeling: Some Current Developments," in Paruchuri R. Krishnaiah (Ed.), *Multivariate Analysis* (Vol. 3, pp. 383-407). New York: Academic Press.

Wold, H. (1985). Partial Least Squares. In S. Kotz & N. L. Johnson (Eds.), *Encyclopedia of Statistical Sciences* (Vol. 6, pp. 581–591). New York: John Wiley & Sons.

Wong, K. K. (2010, Nov). Handling small survey sample size and skewed dataset with partial least square path modelling. *Vue: the magazine of the Marketing Research and Intelligence Association*, 20-23.

Wong, K. K. (2011). Review of the book *Handbook of Partial Least Squares: Concepts, Methods and Applications*, by V. Esposito Vinzi, W.W. Chin, J. Henseler & H. Wang (Eds). *International Journal of Business Science & Applied Management.* 6 (2), 52-54.

Wong, K. K. (2013). Partial Least Squares Structural Equation Modeling (PLS-SEM) Techniques Using SmartPLS. *Marketing Bulletin*, 24, Technical Note 1, 1-32.

Wong, K. K. (2016). Mediation analysis, categorical moderation analysis, and higher-order constructs modeling in Partial Least Squares Structural Equation Modeling (PLS-SEM): A B2B Example using SmartPLS, *Marketing Bulletin*, 26, Technical Note 1, 1-22.

SUBJECT INDEX

Printed in the United States
By Bookmasters